Making Sense Philosophy behind the Headlines

By the same author

Philosophy: Key Texts
Philosophy: Key Themes
The Philosopher's Toolkit (with Peter S. Fosl)
New British Philosophy: The Interviews (ed. with Jeremy Stangroom)

Making Sense
Philosophy Behind the Headlines

Julian Baggini

OXFORD
UNIVERSITY PRESS

Great Clarendon Street, Oxford ox2 6DP

Oxford University Press is a department of the University of Oxford.
It furthers the University's objective of excellence in research, scholarship,
and education by publishing worldwide in

Oxford New York

Auckland Bangkok Buenos Aires Cape Town Chennai
Dar es Salaam Delhi Hong Kong Istanbul Karachi Kolkata
Kuala Lumpur Madrid Melbourne Mexico City Mumbai Nairobi
São Paulo Shanghai Singapore Taipei Tokyo Toronto

with an associated company in Berlin

Oxford is a registered trade mark of Oxford University Press
in the UK and in certain other countries

Published in the United States
by Oxford University Press Inc., New York

British Library Cataloguing in Publication Data
Data available

Library of Congress Cataloging in Publication Data
Data available

ISBN 0–19–280339–5

1 3 5 7 9 10 8 6 4 2

Typeset by RefineCatch Ltd, Bungay, Suffolk
Printed in Great Britain by T.J. International Ltd, Padstow, Cornwall

With love for **Susannah**,
whose lack of blind faith was inspirational.

Acknowledgements

Thanks are especially due to: **Jeremy Stangroom** for extensive comments on an earlier draft of this book; **Lizzy Kremer**, whose comments and suggestions were essential to the book taking its final form; **Shelley Cox** for ensuring it saw the light of day; and **Mary Worthington** for ruthlessly eliminating stray traces of shoddy English.

Contents

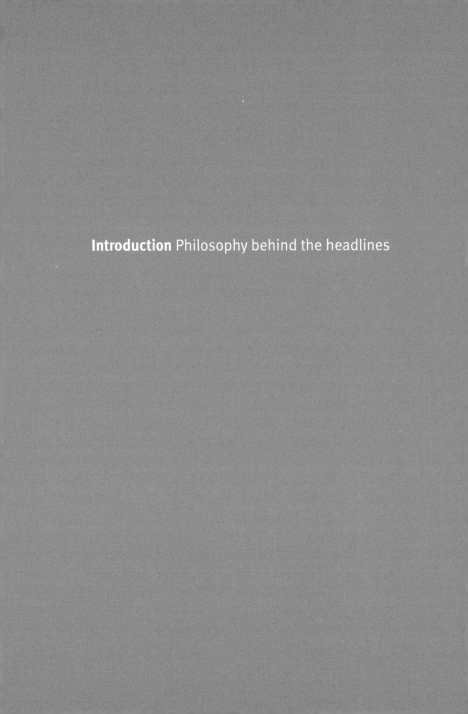

Introduction Philosophy behind the headlines

When the idea for a book examining the philosophy behind the news first entered my mind, the news media was as usual full of philosophically fertile stories:

- In Britain, there were increasing calls for genetically modified foodstuffs to be banned. These products were christened by the popular press 'Frankenstein foods'.
- The manager of the England football team resigned after allegedly saying in an interview that disability is the pay-back for wrongs committed in a previous life.
- The Labour government in Britain, following the new Democrats in the USA, unveiled new reforms to welfare, partially justifying them with its slogan 'no rights without responsibilities'.
- In Yugoslavia, NATO forces engaged in a conflict aimed at bringing about the end of ethnic cleansing in Kosovo, which led to the greatest exodus of people from their homelands since the Second World War.
- The presenter of a long-running children's television programme was sacked after admitting being a regular user of cocaine. The programme makers apologized to their viewers for letting them down.

A few years later and these stories still have a familiar ring. They encompass themes which can be found perennially behind the headlines of the day. War, conflict, drugs, religion, science, and nature are recurrent issues in our newspapers and television bulletins. How does philosophy relate to all of this?

There is a lot of nonsense talked about the relationship between philosophy and the concerns of real life. On the one hand, people who don't seem to have much understanding of what philosophy is chastise philosophers for not addressing the needs of real people. Carrying around some weird image of philosophers as sage gurus or spiritual leaders, they don't seem to realize that the vast majority of modern philosophy is technical, specialized, and as relevant to the concerns of everyday life as theoretical physics.

Equally absurd, however, are those who refuse to see any connection between philosophy as studied in universities and the world around them. On the contrary, behind all the news stories described above lie philosophical problems of enduring and central importance.

Take the first example of genetically modified food. In and among the various important arguments as to the safety of these products there frequently appeared, even in the more serious press, a critical neglect of important philosophical questions and distinctions. For example, since Hume, most philosophers have agreed that just because something is 'natural' that doesn't necessarily mean it is right or good. A little reflection shows this cannot be the case. We frequently do what is not natural without there being any reason to suppose it is wrong to do so. Using the phone or taking an aspirin are just two mundane examples. Conversely, what is natural is often violently resisted. Disease and high rates of infant mortality are both as natural as night turning to day, yet no one would suppose we should therefore rejoice in them. Yet not too far under the surface of the GM foods debate, the error of arguing that the unnaturalness of these foods somehow makes them automatically bad or suspicious frequently reared its head. I consider this and other ways in which philosophy can help us think about the environment in Chapter 6.

A second confusion arises from a lack of understanding of the nature of proof. A reason for banning GM foods frequently cited was that there was not yet firm proof that they were safe. Yet what counts as an adequate proof? Could the safety of GM foods be proved beyond all doubt and if not, what standard of proof is appropriate? These are questions about establishing the truth and about what we can know to be the case. Such questions are always cropping up in the news, which is often led by new scientific research or concerns about pollutants. Questions about the basis of knowledge claims are fundamental to philosophy and are discussed further in Chapter 1.

The whole issue of GM foods also throws up questions about the nature of science. Does science cause more harm than good? Should science stick to examining the world and stop trying to change it? How reliable is scientific knowledge? In an age where we are increasingly calling our scientists to account, I believe our attitudes to science are confused and contradictory. How philosophy can help clarify the way science is viewed in the media is the subject of Chapter 5, where I look at the news coverage of the BSE crisis and human therapeutic cloning.

The resignation of the England football coach after some controversial remarks concerning reincarnation is also a subject infused with philosophy, quite apart from the issue of whether his remarks were offensive to the disabled. The doctrine of reincarnation is one of the world's most popular religious beliefs, and one which has also found credence with many in the West, along with the 'what goes around comes around' belief in

Karma. Many believe that reincarnation is a means by which we could go on to live after our deaths. If this is to make sense as a doctrine, certain ideas about the nature of who we are follow. These ideas have been examined rigorously by philosophers and in Chapter 9 I discuss how they can help clarify our ideas about life, death, and personhood in the context of ongoing controversies about embryo research and allowing patients in persistent vegetative states to die.

In politics, we are now told by both left and right that we have no rights without responsibilities. This can be used to justify taking away automatic rights of people to claim benefits, unless they fulfil their side of the bargain by meeting their responsibilities. Philosophers could have a field day with such a bold statement. On the one hand, it can be persuasively argued that it is simply not true that all rights entail responsibilities. After all, we generally believe that children, the severely mentally ill, the senile, and even perhaps animals have rights, yet do we seriously believe that they too have responsibilities, and that if they don't meet them their rights should be removed? I would presume not. So at the very least, the link between rights and responsibilities is a lot more complicated than the slogan 'no rights without responsibilities' suggests.

More fundamentally, what are rights? Where do they come from? Are rights 'natural'—things we are born with—or are they granted by society on its members? Sometimes they seem to be the former—everyone appears to have the right to life, for example. But even if this is the case, can rights be taken away? If someone kills other people, do they forfeit their rights? And what if we reject the idea of 'natural' rights? Where does that leave our everyday belief in rights? These are basic yet profound questions of political philosophy and because politicians, pressure groups, and commentators so often invoke rights in their campaigns, it is political philosophy which is very important for a serious consideration of the news agenda.

In Chapter 3, issues of rights will come up in relation to two other political concepts invoked in real-life politics that require philosophical analysis: freedom and equality. These issues are discussed in the context of the cynicism and media criticism of new Labour in Britain and the new Democrats in the USA.

What about war? Despite fifty years of relative peace in Western Europe, armed conflicts involving Western nations have occurred all too frequently in recent years. The Falklands, Grenada, the Gulf, Yugoslavia, and Afghanistan are but five such theatres of conflict in the last twenty-five years. Time and time again our countries go to war, each time we agonize over whether or not the war is just, but every time the debate lags behind action on the ground. Kosovo in particular made people think perhaps harder than at any time since the Second World War about the dilemmas facing a country with the choice of diplomacy or military action. Philosophy may not provide the solutions to these agonizing choices, but it can help clarify the issues at stake, as I hope Chapter 4 demonstrates, where the War against Terrorism provides the focus for discussion.

Finally, is it right that a young man should lose his job because, in his own private life, he chooses to take recreational drugs? What fundamentally makes drug use wrong, if indeed it is wrong? And to what extent, if any, are the things a person does in their private life a matter for ethics or public concern? This last issue is discussed in the context of the Clinton–Lewinsky saga in Chapter 2, while the question of how far it is acceptable to limit people's freedom to choose what they want to do is covered in Chapter 3.

Behind the five news stories I mentioned, then, lie a whole barrage of philosophical issues and controversies which have a direct impact on how we understand and respond to them. So the idea that philosophy does relate to the everyday concerns reflected in the news is not a fanciful one at all. The goal of this book is simply to try to show as clearly as possible what some of those relations are.

———————

This book is then about the relationship between philosophy and the real world of current affairs. Before beginning, however, we have to be very clear about what we mean by philosophy and what the relationship between it and real life is.

When I talk about philosophy I am referring to a tradition of thought that can be traced back to the Ancient Greeks and which provides the literature for the academic study of philosophy in Western universities. Of course, this is not the only way to define 'philosophy'. Anyone can have a 'philosophy of life' and this broad sense of philosophy—meaning a certain world-view or way of living—is a legitimate one. Such 'philosophies' are obviously supposed to inform real-life debate, but they are not the subject of this book. Philosophy as studied in Western universities is something quite different, and that is why the criticism which is so often laid at the feet of academic philosophers—that they don't tell us how to live any more—is misconceived. It confuses the popular sense of philosophy with its more technical, academic one.

So what is philosophy, as understood by academic philosophers? One answer, given by G. E. Moore, consisted of simply pointing to his philosophy books and saying, 'It is what all these are about'. The problem with such 'ostensive definitions' is that you first have to read all the books to find out what the word means and even then you may have no clear idea what makes those books part of a single discipline. A more helpful way of defining philosophy is to distinguish between the subject matter of philosophy and its methods.

What makes something a subject for philosophy cannot be specified in precise terms, but such subjects do share what Wittgenstein called a 'family resemblance', which has two particularly striking features. To see how this is so, let us take one example of a philosophical question: What is justice?

The first feature of this question is that it cannot be answered by observation and experiment. What stands between me and an answer is not a lack of scientific studies into the properties of just actions, nor a lack of experience of justice in my life. There is something faintly absurd about imagining that such a question could be answered by a thorough scientific research programme. In short, we are unlikely to arrive at an answer to the question simply by acquiring more facts about the world.

Interestingly, many media discussions do tend to rush to draw philosophical conclusions from the emergence of new facts. For example, when it was announced in June 2000 that the recently completed mapping of the human genome showed it contained fewer genes than was anticipated, many commentators immediately claimed that this somehow meant we did have free will after all, since there could not be a gene for every facet of our natures. Putting to one side the terrible scientific mistakes made by such an analysis, which gets wrong the whole idea of a 'gene for' something, logically the conclusion does not follow. If fewer genes meant more freedom, then we would have to say flies and amoeba have more free will than humans. The remarkable fact that so many noted media commentators missed this obvious point shows how urgent the need for a more philosophically informed media is.

The second feature of a philosophical question, such as 'what is justice?', is that it is of a very general nature. It is not about why *this* action or system is just or what seems just to me: it is rather a question about what justice itself is. Many philosophical questions are similarly general in nature: Philosophers seek to understand such notions as consciousness, right and wrong, causation, and truth.

Put these together and you have some idea of what makes a question philosophical: it is concerned with questions of a general nature which cannot be settled by a mere investigation into the facts.

However, you're not yet 'doing' philosophy unless you bring to these questions a philosophical approach. What characterizes this is an emphasis on intellectual analysis, using as its primary tool rational thought.

It must be remembered that this is not the only way to approach philosophy's subject matter. One could, for example, try to discover the truth by trying to access alternative states of consciousness through meditation. Another alternative is to accept a solution based on authority. This is how some religious believers will arrive at answers to questions of right and wrong, for example. This is why it is important to see how philosophy is a combination of both subject matter *and* method. The method without a subject matter is empty; the subject matter without the method is not what we call philosophy.

I have talked about 'the philosophical approach' as if it were one thing. There are in fact a large number of philosophical approaches, each characterized by their own particular versions of the method of philosophy. But so long as they share this stress on clarity of thought and argumentation, they are philosophical. This means that, despite the differences between them, Anglo-Saxon and 'continental' versions of philosophy are both still essentially philosophy. When it comes to other traditions, such as the many different philosophies which we crudely lump together under the heading 'Eastern Philosophy', things become less clear. Certainly, a lot of Eastern philosophies are more like religions than Western ones. They offer world-views and advice on how to live, but they do not always adopt the philosophical approach I have outlined. That doesn't make them worthless, but it is important to realize that it does make them something other than philosophy as understood in Western society. Of course, I am not suggesting that literally everything that goes under the heading of Western philosophy has the character I have described and that nothing that goes under the name of Eastern philosophy does, but there are general differences of approach and they must be recognized. It also means that relating Western and Eastern philosophy is a difficult, and perhaps hopeless, task.

Having clarified, a little at least, what is meant by philosophy, we now need to consider how it relates to the real-world concerns of the news media. My claim that philosophy is of use here is not the claim that the arguments and ideas of academic philosophers usually provide practical pearls of wisdom and guides for life. One only needs to read a few pages of a modern philosophy journal to see this is not true. This book is not an introduction to academic philosophy, nor is it a guide to how academic philosophy can help you live your life. The value philosophy has to real-world debates is mostly in the extent to which we can use its methods and the insights of its great figures to help us understand better the kinds of general philosophical questions that lie behind the headlines of the day.

Consider the methods first. Philosophy has no monopoly on rationality, but because of its emphasis and reliance on sound reasoning and its examination of the principles of reasoning themselves, one probably learns more about what makes a good, rational argument from philosophy than from any other subject. This is extremely valuable in real-world debate. The ability to see the form and strength of an argument can prevent us from being confused or misled by those who know how to manipulate us. When we decide whether or not we should take out insurance, or bet all our money on the national lottery, or have an immunization jab, the most reliable way of deciding is to consider the rational arguments for and against. If we act purely out of instinct or on our emotions, we are very unlikely to make the right decision about any of these things.

So philosophy, by training the mind and helping us to think better, is of great use in helping us to understand the complex issues behind the headlines. But if this were all it were useful for, doing it would be like working out in a mental gym. We (well, not me) pump iron and run on treadmills to get fit, not because we want to lift bits of metal or run on the spot. In a similar way, it could be thought that, when we do philosophy, we are working to get our minds fit, not because we really want to know the answers to philosophical questions. If that were true, philosophy would still have a value in understanding contemporary debates. But I think philosophy has a greater value than this, because there are specifically philosophical questions we do come across in the news every day, as I outlined in the first part of this introduction. To make sense of the news, and the world around us, we all have to confront, at some stage, questions such as those of right and wrong, our conception of self, and the status of scientific claims. These are properly philosophical questions because of their generality and because they are not questions that require mere facts to be answered. Academic philosophy, with two millennia of history behind it, considers such questions at a high level of abstraction, and it is very rare for anyone who hasn't studied philosophy long and hard and who has an exceptional talent to make a real contribution to the growth of academic philosophy. But, nonetheless, we can help ourselves to the philosophical approach to help address the kinds of questions that are thrown up just by the process of living.

Finally, a few words of warning. I claim no particular originality for the arguments presented in this book. In a sense, their value is that they are *not* original. Rather they are the kinds of arguments which recur time and again when anyone adopts a philosophical attitude to events in the world. At the same time this is not a neutral account of what philosophers think. Philosophers disagree and what I offer here is one person's view. I have tried to be fair, but where it seems to me that an argument is particularly strong or weak my convictions shine through. The purpose of this book is to open up and reveal the philosophical issues and arguments behind the news, not to convince you of my own views. But my views are here and I both hope and expect that this is a book you will want to argue with rather than accept lock, stock, and barrel. I do not intend this book as the last word but as an invitation for more philosophizing to begin.

BIN LADEN, ON TAPE, BOASTS OF TRADE CENTER ATTACKS; U.S. SAYS IT PROVES HIS GUILT

Truth, lies, and videotape: The problem of knowledge

What's going on?

In 2001 Britain and America went to war. This was a 'war against terrorism' with several enemies. The explicit though elusive target of the first campaign of this war was the terrorist network al-Qaeda and its bases in Afghanistan. The Taliban regime in Afghanistan, an alleged state sponsor of terrorism, also became a target owing to its refusal to 'hand over' Osama bin Laden, the leader of al-Qaeda, who had his headquarters in the country. Relatively few British or American lives were directly at risk in this campaign.

In the UK, the media coverage of this conflict was, in historical terms at least, surprisingly mixed. Little more than twenty years ago, when Britain had gone to war with Argentina over the Falkland Islands—Las Malvinas—the media mood was generally jingoistic. There was of course some dissent, but overall it was clear who the good and the bad guys were supposed to be.

Go back even further to the Second World War and the differences are even more marked. The government propaganda films of the day strike modern viewers as almost comical in their simplicity. They present a simple world-view where the brave and noble allies are the enemies of the evil Hun. What is more, the average civilian, reading the newspapers or watching the newsreels, generally seemed to accept without question the official information put out by government departments.

In the war against terrorism, by contrast, there was much more questioning. For example, early in 2002, the *Mirror*, a populist British tabloid, devoted its front page to questioning the effectiveness of the military campaign. Such a move in a popular paper when, from a British point of view, the campaign seemed to be going pretty well and there had been no British casualties to date, would once have been unthinkable. In the more serious broadsheet press, the lack of a clear consensus in the comment pages was more predictable. But even here the range of divergent opinions and the depth of the questioning was unusual.

Of course, some of these differences can be accounted for in terms of the very different natures of the various conflicts. But it also seems to be the case that the different reactions are in part due to an important change in public attitudes. We are now more sceptical, both of our governments and our media. We no longer trust either to present us with the truth. We chew over what they tell us rather than swallow it whole. In short, the public is much less naive than it used to be. We want to know what's going on but don't seem to be able to trust any of the sources that might tell us.

This deep questioning which has gone on in the media is not just a consequence of a loss of innocence. There are also several important philosophical issues mixed up in the various discussions of the rights and wrongs of the campaign. Some of these concern the morality of war, and I will look at these in Chapter 4. Others, however, concern issues of truth and knowledge. These are the subject of the present chapter.

The acuteness of Arthur Ponsonby's observation that truth is the first casualty of war is not diminished by its becoming a cliché. In times of conflict governments and other agents are very keen to control the information flow in order to keep the civilian population on side or the international community at bay. Consider, for instance, how wildly different were Israeli and

Palestinian accounts of the alleged massacre at the Jenin refugee camp in April 2002. This means that knowing what the truth is in times of war can be extremely difficult. If we want to know the extent of civilian casualties, how prisoners of war are being treated or what the real threat of further terrorist attacks are—all vital for making a judgement as to the rights or wrongs of the war—we need accurate information. But what are our chances of knowing the truth about any of these when the best source of information—government intelligence—comes to us through the filter of political propaganda? Without some kind of guide for distinguishing truth from falsehood, we are lost.

There is a second difficulty, which is more fundamental. The problem here is that there seem to be what we might call competing truth claims. For instance, on the one hand, there are those who believe that America was attacked without provocation by a band of terrorists with no respect for liberty and human life. On the other, there are those, particularly in places like Palestine, who believe that American imperialism has repeatedly attacked Islam in the Middle East and that al-Qaeda is part of a holy struggle to save the region from American domination. The worry here is not that we can't tell which account is true. It is rather that there is no one truth—instead one set of facts is true for some people and another true for others. It just depends on how you look at it.

There are many such competing truth claims. Was the tape of Bin Laden 'confessing' to the 11 September attacks real or genuine? Were the Taliban prisoners killed at the fort near Mazar-i-Sharif the victims of an atrocity or did they just lose out in a battle to escape? Were the Taliban prisoners held in American detention camps in Guantanamo Bay, Cuba mistreated and denied basic human rights or just temporarily shackled for security reasons? In all of these cases, the worry is not that we do not know the truth, but that there is no single truth there at all. What the truth is depends on through whose eyes you are looking at things.

The branch of philosophy which considers questions about truth and knowledge is known as epistemology or, more prosaically, the theory of knowledge. Two of the central issues of epistemology have a direct bearing on these responses to the news about a conflict such as the war against terrorism. In broad terms, these are questions, first, about the status or nature of truth itself and, second, about our relationship to that truth.

The first issue is the more fundamental. What is at stake here is whether or not there exists a single, objective truth or whether it is more accurate to say that there is a plurality of 'truths' or even no truth at all, only opinion. The first view can be termed realist because it asserts that the truth exists whether we know it or not: the truth is real and independent of us. For the second view we have to be content with the name non-realist, for only this term covers the wide range of different positions all opposed to realism. On this view, the idea that the truth exists independently of us, just waiting to be discovered, is intellectually unsophisticated. Truth is never just 'out there'. Truths are always in some way created, by language, society, individuals, or cultures.

These somewhat academic-sounding concerns may sound a long way from media coverage of the war against terrorism. But I would argue that the tendency for forms of non-realism to become the orthodoxy in many 'educated' circles has contributed to the uncertainty over responses to the anti-terrorism campaign. If there is no one truth, then the best we can do in this conflict is to list the various competing 'truths' which are believed by the opposing sides. So, for example, members of the al-Qaeda network see themselves as following God's will; many Americans believe it is they who have God on their side. Some see the civilian casualties in Afghanistan as being a form of intentional murder; others see them as unintentional 'collateral damage'. Some see American incursions into Afghanistan as breeches of international law; others see it as in line with the laws of self-defence. The list could go on.

Of course, very few people are explicitly non-realists about truth. But many features of non-realism have infused the way many of us think today. At the very least, it introduces a series of doubts into people's minds as they consider the distant conflict: Who are we to say who is right and who is wrong? Who are we to say what 'the truth' about this conflict is?

This profound unease about the very possibility of a single truth is accompanied by a less fundamental, but no less important unease about our relationship to the truth. Let us suppose for a moment that non-realism does not affect our thinking. We believe there is one truth and that truth is 'out there'. Nevertheless, there is still another problem: how can we know what that truth is? We are confronted with so many different, competing claims for truth. How can we sort through these and discover the real truth buried underneath? If we are sceptical about the possibility of finding out what the real truth is, then we can be left as uncertain about a conflict such as the war against terrorism as we would be if we rejected the very idea of truth itself.

These concerns about truth and knowledge affect the way we read about any news story. If we do not believe it is possible for news stories to be true and objective, why should we bother with them at all? The problem, however, is not only one for the non-realists and sceptics. Even if we are not sceptical about the very possibility of truth and knowledge about world events, we still need some way of distinguishing between truth and falsity, knowledge and opinion. And we also need some way of answering those who would view our belief in truth and knowledge as being outmoded, naive, and simplistic.

I believe these questions are important for several reasons. For one, it seems to be an undeniable fact about human beings that they care about the truth. The desire for the truth to be acknowledged can become the issue of most importance in people's lives. In South Africa after apartheid, it was felt truth was more important than even justice, and so partial immunity was granted to those prepared to testify to the truth. People wrongly convicted of crimes will seek to clear their names even after they are released. And on a more mundane level, having untruths told about oneself is one of the most infuriating and hurtful things that can happen. So despite the sceptical doubts we may have about the possibility of finding truth, the fact that we care about it is one reason why we should try to understand what it is as clearly as possible.

Secondly, we live in the 'information age' and we are bombarded all the time with various conflicting and competing claims for truth and knowledge. Some people deny the holocaust, others assert it happened as a matter of undeniable fact. Some say they know that Jesus is Lord, others say that atheism is the true view. Some people say that scientists know we are nothing more than biological organisms while others say our true selves are spiritual and still others say scientists know nothing at all—it's all just their point of view. From time to time we may throw our hands up and say, 'maybe they're all right' but more often than not, we make a choice between competing truth claims. Some of these choices are very important, others less so. But we make them all the time, and having some understanding of the meaning of truth and knowledge can only help us choose more wisely.

Truth first

As knowledge seems to depend on truth and not the other way around, it makes sense to start with truth. The view that there is no one truth is a remarkably popular one. Indeed, teaching introductory philosophy classes, I have had students say to me that they assumed this was what all philosophers now think. As it turns out, philosophers believe many different things about truth, some of which are certainly non-realist. Since the Ancient Greek philosopher Protagoras proclaimed that 'Man is the measure of all things' there have always been philosophers who it would be accurate to describe as relativists. But very few of these relativisms boil down to the belief that no 'truths' are superior or inferior to any other, or that truth is simply what people happen to believe. It is this crude version of relativism about truth which I am concerned with here, not its more sophisticated philosophical cousins. On this view there is no one truth, rather truth is always relative to a society, individual, or culture. Put another way, things are never true, period, and that makes it pointless even to talk about unqualified truth. Things are always true *for* someone, some society, or some culture. It may be true *for you* that Bin Laden is a terrorist, but it is true *for others* that he is a holy warrior. It may be true *for you* that America is a benign world-policeman, but it is true *for others* that it is a neo-imperialistic power.

On a radio programme not long ago, I heard a professor of English defend the claim that truth is relative using the example of Columbus. He asked whether it is true that Columbus discovered America. He claimed that while this is true for the conquistadors, it clearly wasn't true for the native Americans. Hence, he argued, what's true for some people is not true for others. In this way, he was endorsing the popular relativist view of truth I described above: there is no truth, period, only truth for someone, some culture, or some society.

A parallel argument can be constructed for the campaign in Afghanistan. Consider the incident at the fort near Mazar-i-Sharif. Here, according to the Northern Alliance troops who held the Taliban captives, more than 400 prisoners were killed because they started an uprising and could only be stopped with violence. According to the Taliban, the uprising was caused by the fact that the prisoners had been mistreated and the Northern Alliance was over-zealous in quashing it. So if we ask the question, were the prisoners fairly treated, we might say that is true for the captors but not for the captives. There is no one truth.

Both these arguments seem to me to be terrible pieces of

reasoning. The arguments move from the mere fact that people have different opinions to the conclusion that truth is relative. We are asked to accept that because the native American and the conquistadors, the Northern Alliance and the Taliban, *believed* different things to be true, there is no one truth. But instead of demonstrating that this is the case, these arguments merely assume it. It is obvious that the mere fact that people disagree about the truth doesn't prove there is more than one truth. All it shows is that people disagree. If we disagree about what the capital of Australia is, it doesn't therefore follow that Australia has two capitals. In this case, it is clear that one of us is in fact wrong.

All these examples show is that the same event can have two different descriptions and that these descriptions may seem to conflict. In the Americas case, it is quite clear that the conflict only occurs at the level of description—there is no disagreement about the underlying facts. Both the conquistadors and the native Americans knew full well that the native Americans were there first. The conquistadors weren't that stupid. The reason why there is a disagreement is that what was a discovery for the conquistadors was not a discovery for the native Americans. A discovery is when one learns for the first time that something is true. To say Columbus discovered America is to say therefore that Columbus was the first European to find out that America existed, a fact the native Americans knew already. So the difference between the natives and the conquistadors is not that there are two truths out there. It is rather that there is one truth out there—America exists—and one group knew that while the other previously had not.

So the idea that there was one truth for the conquistadors and one for the native Americans turns out to be a very superficial one. It only seems to be a respectable view if we take the different ways of describing the event at face value. When we look closer we find not only that there is one true set of facts, but that both groups would actually agree about what they were: There was a continent that had been inhabited for a very long time and Columbus was the first European to go there.

In the case of the Mazar-i-Sharif uprising, there are two disagreements. One is about how we judge what went on. Perhaps both parties could agree on the sequence of events, but still one side would judge that the captors behaved fairly, the other that they behaved barbarically. The same point arises here as it does when we consider facts. The mere fact that the two parties disagree about whether an action is fair or unfair is not enough to show that both parties are right. The existence of different views about morality no more shows that morality is relative than the existence of different views about what the facts are shows that truth is relative.

But even if we do want to end up saying that there is no objective way of telling who is right about what is morally fair, this still does not lead to the conclusion that truth is relative, since the questions of what is moral and what is factually correct are separate. It is perfectly possible to accept moral relativism while rejecting epistemic relativism—relativism about truth. So, for example, one might say that there is a single truth about what actually happened at Mazar-i-Sharif, but there is no single truth as to whether or not what happened was morally justifiable.

Moral 'truth' can be—and arguably should be—kept separate from factual truth.

The second disagreement concerning Mazar-i-Sharif, however, is about the facts, since the two parties do not actually agree about what the sequence of events was. But this does not mean that both alleged sets of facts about what happened are true. If we were able to see all that went on at Mazar-i-Sharif over the three days of the uprising we would be in a position to tell which account was correct. The fact that we don't know which account is right (or might be wrong when we judge which is false) does not mean that there is more than one truth.

Consider the conquistadors again. What if Columbus wasn't the first European to visit the Americas? If the Vikings had got there first, would that mean that the statement 'Columbus was the first European to visit America' is true for us, but not true for the Vikings? It would not. All it would mean is that we were wrong. In other words, it shows we may be wrong to think we know the truth, not that there may be more than one truth. Whether there is a single truth and whether we can claim to know the truth are two different questions. The first concerns what is, the second what we know. If we ignore this difference, we cannot make sense of the distinction between what we *think* is true and what *is* true.

If we do not make this distinction we soon end up with nonsense. If everything we think to be true is true, or there is no difference between the two, then that means we can never be in error. To believe this is to fly away with the fairies. For example, it is very possible to think today is Wednesday when really it is

Thursday. But if there is no difference between what I think is true and what is true, then if I think today is Wednesday it is Wednesday, and damn the calendar. If I arrive late for work, I can simply say, 'It may be true for you that I'm late, but it's true for me that I'm early.' Such a state of affairs would be absurd. Not only would it be impractical and unworkable, I doubt whether anyone could seriously believe it. When you arrive late for work and make your excuses that truth is relative, I am certain that not too deep down you would think that, actually, you really were late.

If the absurdity and impracticality of this view is not enough to convince you it is wrong, then ask yourself if you could believe the following: it is true for some people that six million people were killed in the holocaust but it is not true for others. It is no more true to say that the world is spherical than it is to say it is flat. The view that there is life after death and that death is the end are both equally true. I would say that to agree with these statements is to give up on all rational discourse. There would be no point in discussing anything with someone who believed these things, because, in effect, they have agreed to suspend all judgement on anything. Of course, if we say 'true for me' just means 'what I believe' then it is trivially true that 'what's true for me may not be true for you'. But we must accept that there is another use of true, without the qualification 'for me, you, him, or them', which is more serious than this one. This use of true may turn out to be complex and involve elements of relativism, but it is not the crude relativism currently so popular in society and in some sections of academia.

We should now be able to see that it is too simplistic to say that it may be true *for you* that God is not on Bin Laden's side, but it is true *for others* that he is; or that it may be true *for you* that al-Qaeda's suicide killers are now in heaven, but it is true *for others* that they are most certainly not. In some cases there are questions of moral judgement which may admit of disagreement. But there are many more facts which are not just matters of opinion. We may ultimately disagree as to whether or not to class Osama bin Laden as a terrorist. But before we reach that point we should be able to accept that the facts which we use as the basis for these judgements are truths that hold for everyone, not just some people. These facts concern what actually Bin Laden and America have done, what is actually written in the Koran, how the major players in this campaign have formed their decisions and so on. There is nothing relative about any of these facts. They may be hard to ascertain, but that does not make them any less objective and real.

The attractions of relativism

Before moving on, it may be worth thinking about why this view has become so popular in recent years. I think that the reasons that explain its popularity are a lot more important than the view itself. Consider the appeal of relativism when trying to understand why it is that people willingly join al-Qaeda and martyr themselves for its benefit. To have any chance of understanding this, it is important to suspend judgement on the people and societies we are thinking about and really to try to get within their world-view and understand it. While it may make sense, however, to suspend judgement for research purposes, that does not mean that we should suspend judgement on cool reflection afterwards.

But there is another motivation at work here: respect for diversity of opinion. We live in a multi-cultural world where many groups have many different conceptions of reality and truth. Indeed, countries like Britain have large Muslim minorities, some, perhaps many, of whom have very different worldviews from those of the typical white liberal. It is vital that these points of view are listened to with respect. To impose our view (whoever 'we' may be) on everyone else seems colonialist, arrogant, and unfair. So it seems far better to accept everyone's version of the truth than fascistically to impose our own. We have had too much experience in the last century of the horrors of totalitarianism to presume there is one right way that all must follow.

If I describe these motives as noble I do not do so in any patronizing sense. But what we have to acknowledge here is that what we are really saying is that it is politically and socially undesirable to impose one view of the truth on everyone—it does not mean that there *is* no one truth. We are also saying that it is arrogant to presume that one has a *unique insight* into the truth, which is again different from saying there is no one truth. What we need to be afraid of is not that there is one truth, but that we might wrongly believe we have grasped that truth completely and impose it on other people. Both would be mistakes. One of the greatest of all philosophers, Socrates, is supposed to have said that the only thing he knew was that he knew nothing. Those who are most convinced that they are absolutely right are often those who are most terribly wrong. We are right to be suspicious of any group or individual who claim to know the whole truth, but that does not mean there *is* no one truth.

The other mistake is to impose by force our view of the truth on others. This is usually wrong for the reason just given, namely, that we are often mistaken about what we suppose to be true. But even if we were right, there seems little reason to believe that much good can come from imposing the truth on people. People will not see the truth through coercion and arguably it is better that people are wrong but free (so long as their ignorance does not harm others) than that they are forced to accept the truth. Political fascism is a disastrous policy, even when the fascist leader knows the truth.

So at the root of our love affair with relativism are two well-grounded beliefs: that we should not be arrogant about our claims to knowledge and truth and that it is wrong to impose our view of the truth on others. Neither of these views logically leads to the conclusion that there is no truth, but nonetheless many do make this leap, spurred on by the desire to respect the different beliefs of others. I have tried to argue that, all the same, it is disastrous to make this leap, which leaves us unable to distinguish truth from fiction, belief from knowledge, and opinion from fact.

One final point about relativism about truth: one reason we are attracted to it is because we know that people are different, and what may be good for some people may not be good for others. So, for example, arranged marriages might suit some people but not others. Some might flourish within the comforts of a traditional religion, others with non-belief. Some want to live with extended families, others with nuclear families, some on their own. We feel that if there is one truth, then we have to give up this diversity. That does not follow. Truths about facts or states of affairs are different from statements of values or life-style preferences. The statement 'what suits me may not suit you' is entirely different from the statement 'what's true for me may not be true for you'. The view that there is such a thing as the truth does not mean that there is just one way to live. The two issues are distinct. So we need not fear that accepting there is one truth about matters of fact leads to a kind of cultural imperialism where all diversity of lifestyle is eradicated.

Back to the war

What does this all mean for the war on terrorism in general? My suspicion is that at least some of the reaction to the war is con-fused because of an ill-thought-out attitude to truth. But we are right to be suspicious of the various versions of the truth that are presented to us. We are right to think that the real truth can be hard to uncover. We are right to want to respect the perspectives of other people and to, as far as is possible, incorporate them into our understanding of the situation. We are right to believe that the truth can appear to be very different depending on where you are looking at it from. We might be right to think that we should not export our values into countries that have differ-ent moral codes. But none of this is at all incompatible with the view that some of what is reported is true and some of it is false, and that there is no need to say for whom it is true or false: it is true or false for everyone.

The problem is not that people explicitly—or even

consciously—hold non-realist views. Most people would agree that the USA did or did not bomb a warehouse in Kabul run by the Red Cross in October 2001; that Bin Laden had or had not already left Afghanistan by the time Operation Enduring Peace began in the same month; and that the Afghan Northern Alliance did or did not deliberately kill 400 prisoners of war at Mazar-i-Sharif. When applied to specific facts, the non-realist position is just too counter-intuitive to appeal to many people. My view is rather that a much vaguer commitment to non-realism, especially as concerns moral values, tends to colour our whole way of thinking, so that we find ourselves instinctively withholding judgement. When the truth is hard to ascertain it is much easier to adopt a sceptical stance towards the possibility of truth than it is actually to get to it.

What we need to realize is that, at least when it comes to the facts about events, there is truth and there is falsehood and we need to be able to distinguish between the two. For sophisticated philosophical reasons, you may wish to say that the truth is nonetheless relative in some way and you may wish to reject the simply realist stance. But this does not mean one has to accept that there is no important difference between truth or falsehood or that one needs to adopt the crude version of relativism I have criticized in this chapter. We should not confuse a justifiable desire to avoid imposing one point of view on others with a rejection of the idea of truth. Indeed, to form any sensible judgement at all about the War on Terrorism we need to accept that there are some facts to base these judgements on.

Knowledge

So far we have focused on the idea of truth. It could be argued that I have overestimated the extent to which non-realist ways of understanding truth have permeated the general consciousness. Perhaps most people do think that there is such a thing as 'the truth'. Nonetheless, what many more people do doubt is that we have any chance of knowing what this truth is. Who is to say what happened at Mazar-i-Sharif? Who knows if the Bin Laden videos are authentic? People are sceptical, perhaps not about the existence of truth, but about our ability to know it.

The contemporary American philosopher Thomas Nagel has said that scepticism about knowledge actually requires a realist conception. One can only be truly sceptical about the possibility of knowledge if one believes that there is something real to be known. Only if you accept that there is truth, but then claim we have no way of actually obtaining it, do you arrive at scepticism.

The British philosopher A. J. Ayer distinguished between philosophical and ordinary scepticism. Ordinary scepticism concerns the reliability of particular sources of knowledge. In this sense of the word, if I am sceptical about a daily tabloid newspaper, for example, then I do not believe it is a reliable source of knowledge. Philosophical scepticism, in contrast, is not about particular sources of knowledge, but the general possibility of knowledge. A philosophical sceptic, for example, might believe that it is not possible to obtain any knowledge of the 'external world' and that we can only know about the direct objects of our perception—what we see, hear, taste, touch, and smell. Whether these sensations correspond to an independent reality is something we can never know.

The person who does not believe it is possible truly to know what is going on in the war against terrorism is generally a sceptic in the ordinary sense of the word. Such a person does not normally believe that they cannot know whether material objects in general exist or whether they can know anything at all. Nevertheless, this ordinary scepticism is often motivated by the same kinds of concerns which can lead to philosophical scepticism, and for this reason a consideration of the philosophical response to the sceptical challenge can help provide a response to this ordinary scepticism.

What then does motivate scepticism about knowledge? Consider one example from the war on terrorism that might inspire scepticism. In December 2001 the US government released a video recording which showed Osama bin Laden talking about the attacks on the World Trade Centre three months earlier, in terms which made it clear that he had been behind the attacks. For most, this was the 'smoking gun' which proved Bin Laden's culpability. But some rejected this, saying that the film could have been faked. The poor quality of the soundtrack was taken as suspicious, as was the fact that there seemed no explanation of how the USA had got the tape or why Bin Laden would have agreed to being filmed in the first place.

Let us then assume, having considered the arguments in the first part of this chapter, that there is a truth of the matter here— the video was or was not a fake. The problem many have is that there seems no way we can ever prove the matter one way or another. Without proof, there can be no knowledge of the truth and all we are left with is a difference of opinion.

But this line of reasoning moves too fast and rests upon one of the greatest red herrings in the history of argument: the significance of provability. The man who exposed this red herring was David Hume, and what he said provides the source of what I am going on to say next.

What is required to prove something is true? In law, it is to show that something is true 'beyond reasonable doubt'. What constitutes reasonable doubt is, of course, subject to debate. But there is another sense of proof, which philosophers yearned after for thousands of years—a proof so secure that it was beyond *all*—not just reasonable—doubt.

One problem with this notion of proof is that doubt is a state of mind, and some people find it impossible to doubt things that we all think have *not* been proven (for example, that mobile phone masts cause cancers), while others seem able to doubt things which most believe *are* proven (for example, that humans and apes share a common ancestor). So there is no direct relationship between proof on the one hand, and what we can or cannot doubt on the other. Proof concerns the reasons to accept statements about the world; doubt is about the states of our minds.

Indeed, experience should tell us that certainty is often inversely proportionate to knowledge. The fanatic who believes without question is wrong more often than the sceptic who feels certain about nothing. If knowledge is about what one cannot doubt, then the people who have the greatest claim to knowledge are those members of al-Qaeda who have no doubt that their martyrdom will send them straight to heaven.

So rather than defining proof in terms of what cannot be doubted, most philosophers have thought it more fruitful to look to logic to provide the paradigm case of proof. Something can be logically proved if it can be shown that to deny it leads one to a logical contradiction. A popular example is a simple sum: $1 + 1 = 2$. Given the definitions of '1', '2', '+' and '=', $1 + 1$ must equal 2. To deny this is to contradict yourself. The very meaning of the words themselves ensures that the sum is correct. Perhaps a more graphic example is the statement 'All bachelors are unmarried'. This must be true, because to deny it means to contradict the very meaning of the words used.

This is a simple point but one which is often misunderstood, so have patience with me if I say a little more about it. I have heard people object that it may be true in our world that $1 + 1 = 2$ but that may not be true elsewhere. Similarly, in some countries, maybe bachelors can be married. This objection is mistaken because it assumes that because it is possible that the terms used could be used differently elsewhere, then the statements cannot be proved to be true. Certainly, there could be a country where the word 'bachelor' did not mean 'unmarried man', but all that would mean is that we have a word which both sounds and is written the same way as it is elsewhere, but which means something different. It doesn't show that the way we use 'bachelor', to mean that 'all bachelors are unmarried', is a statement which cannot be known with certainty to be true.

A final worry, which was first expressed by René Descartes in his masterpiece the *Meditations*, is that we may be so mad, deluded, or deceived that even what we think cannot be denied without contradiction may, in fact, be wrong. This form of radical scepticism is hard, if not impossible, to refute. It is logically possible that I am mad, or that I am just dreaming, or that I am a brain in a vat, and all my experiences are the result of an evil scientist manipulating my brain to make me think that I am interacting in the world. But for reasons that should become clear, the mere fact that this is possible is no reason for us to believe that it is actually the case. And there are reasons for believing that to succumb to this kind of radical doubt is to leave us unable to say anything which makes sense at all. Belief that we are not mad or in a constant state of delusion is the bare minimum requirement for attempting to say anything about the world at all.

The concept of proof I have been describing, whereby something is proven to be true if it cannot be denied without logical contradiction, is all very well, but how much can really be proved in this way? Mathematics, geometry, and things true by definition seem provable on this test, but little else. Take the view that the earth orbits the sun. We can deny this without contradicting ourselves. We may have to hypothesize pretty remarkable things to explain why it seems to be that way, but that is not the same as logically contradicting ourselves. The person who claims NASA and the authorities are engaged in a conspiracy to convince us all the world is spherical may be mad, but she is not contradicting herself. In other words, it is logically possible she is right. In the same way, no matter how convoluted a story we have to tell in order to maintain that the Bin Laden tapes were fakes, we need not ever contradict ourselves to tell it. This means it is always a logical possibility that the story is true. The same is true of most, if not all, statements about the way the world actually is. Unlike a statement like '1 + 1 = 2', it is always possible to assert the opposite of such statements without thereby contradicting yourself. Therefore it always remains possible that you could be wrong, and so proof, in this strict sense, is unobtainable.

But just as an inability to prove something is right is no reason to dismiss a theory, so an inability to prove it is wrong is no reason to accept it. Many beliefs cannot be proved wrong. Let's say that right now I claim that there is an invisible pink elephant dancing on your book. It has no weight, no colour, smell, or texture, but it is there. You can't prove I'm not right, in the strict sense of proof we have been discussing! But clearly this is no reason to suppose I am right. Firm proof, both negative and positive, is perhaps always impossible when it comes to statements about the world, so an inability to provide such a proof is neither here nor there.

So if we insist that conclusive proof is required before we accept anything as true, we will never be able to accept any substantive statements about the world as true. Nothing could prove beyond all possible dispute that the Bin Laden tapes are genuine or fakes. This is the reason why the law demands only proof beyond *reasonable* doubt, not all *possible* doubt. Buried beneath the law is the philosophical insight that matters of fact—truths about what actually goes on in our world—can never be proved beyond all possible dispute.

So how do we prove things beyond *reasonable* doubt? As in a court case, we do so by appeal to the evidence. It is on the balance of evidence that we decide whether one view is right or wrong. In assessing the evidence, we can use a method of reasoning known as abduction. Abduction is a term coined by the American pragmatist philosopher Charles Sanders Peirce meaning 'argument to the best explanation'. The idea here is that we are often presented with more than one possible explanation for an event or a state of affairs with no conclusive way of knowing which one is correct. In such instances, all we can hope to do is decide which explanation is best.

In making this decision we can make use of a few principles that people of reason throughout history have seen as reliable. The first, explained with some eloquence by David Hume's discussion of miracles in his *Enquiry Concerning Human Understanding*, is that when an account contradicts other, well-established facts, we must have very good reasons before we accept it as true. For example, when I watch the illusionist David Copperfield 'flying' through the air, this contradicts the well-established fact that people cannot fly unaided. I therefore assume that he is not flying unaided at all, and I would be right to do so. No major 'magician' claims to be performing anything other than illusions. I marvel at his skill, but I don't throw away beliefs about the world which all other experience has shown to be true.

Of course, sometimes we are presented with evidence that challenges established facts and it turns out it is the established facts that are wrong. Such was the case in the third century BC, when people such as Hipparchus claimed the earth was spherical. But if we look a little closer, we will find that the reason why people were wrong to dismiss Hipparchus is because his view actually fitted more of the established facts than the view that the world was flat. It turned out that though Hipparchus' view conflicted with one big and popular view, it fitted in with countless other, better-established facts far better than the one it contradicted. For example, it explained the apparent motion of the sun, stars, *and* planets, and why there is a horizon and why no one has ever fallen off the edge of the world. This is why I said we must have very good reason before accepting a view that contradicts established facts, not that we should never accept such views. Such a policy would simply prevent any progress in human knowledge at all.

Another principle widely accepted is that of economy of explanation. If you have two explanations for an occurrence, the idea is that, all other things being equal, we should always prefer the simpler over the more complex. This principle is known as 'Occam's Razor', after its progenitor, William of Occam. To see why this is a reasonable principle, consider this example: you find a hole in a window the width of one bullet and a bullet in the wall, in line with the hole. One explanation is that a single bullet has been fired through the window. A second explanation is that two bullets were fired through the same hole and that the second bullet has been removed by someone. A third explanation is that one hundred bullets were fired though the same hole, all of which have been removed bar the one in the wall. Which explanation would you go for? It seems only reasonable, all other things being equal, to favour the first. To accept the second you have to accept certain things being true that you have no good reason to believe are true. There is only evidence of one bullet being fired, so why believe there were two? The third option is simply outrageous. Though it is possible it is true, there is no good reason to suppose it is.

Of course, often the real explanation is not the simplest, which is why the clause 'all other things being equal' is important. If it were reported that two shots were heard to fire in quick succession and that there was evidence that someone had entered the room and removed something, that would make us consider the second view. But without this extra evidence, we would be foolish to pursue the two-bullet theory. After all, if we always considered every possible explanation, no matter how outrageous, and without any reason to suppose it is the true one, we would never get anywhere.

A third principle is to prefer the theory which has greater explanatory power. Here's an example from the philosopher Hilary Putnam. A long-standing philosophical puzzle is how we can know other people have minds, given that we cannot look into their heads and see if they are really thinking, feeling, and perceiving. Couldn't other people just be robots or zombies that behave as though they had minds? Putnam's solution to this problem is simply to measure up the two hypotheses. If we assume other people have minds, that explains why it is they talk like they do, act like they do, have the same physiology as us, and so on. If we assume they are robots or zombies, we are left with too many unanswered questions. Nothing in the zombie or robot theory explains why they act the way they do, unless we hypothesize the existence of unseen causes, demonic 'puppet masters', or the like. So given what we do know, the theory that other people have minds has much greater explanatory power than alternative theories. That gives us a good reason to prefer it.

If we combine these principles with our insights into provability, we can now return to the Bin Laden tapes. The demand for conclusive proof that they are genuine can now be seen as a red herring. Rather we should use abduction to see which is the best explanation of the tape's existence on the balance of evidence. To help weigh up this evidence, we can consider which explanation best fits in with the established facts, which is the most economical, and which has the greater explanatory power.

When we apply these principles to the Bin Laden tapes I think we should conclude that the best explanation is that the tapes are genuine. The alternative theory suffers from the same weaknesses as other conspiracy theories. First, it requires us to accept many facts which are not established. This is the strength and weakness of conspiracy theories. They hypothesize huge amounts of suppressed information, which means that the unavailability of the evidence is part of the conspiracy story itself. But while this makes disproving the theories hard, since the evidence isn't available, it leaves us with no reasons actually to accept the theory as true. Second, the explanation is not simple, since it requires us to accept that all sorts of people have been involved in a complex deception and none of this has yet been discovered. In contrast, the explanation that the tape is genuine—though it leaves some questions unanswered—is simple. Third, it leaves many things unexplained—perhaps more than the rival theory—such as why no one has been able to show the tape is a fake, how exactly such a fake was made, and why no other counter-evidence to the tape's authenticity has been uncovered.

Using an abductive method to decide what the truth is does require us to accept some limitations on our knowledge. First, we can often expect, as in this case, that the account we accept will leave some things unexplained. If we accept the tape is genuine, we still don't know how or why the recording was made and how it got into US hands. Incompleteness of explanation just has to be lived with sometimes. What we have to avoid doing is filling in the missing details with wild speculation or making the mistake of supposing that an incomplete explanation is a fundamentally wrong explanation. I cannot explain to you how the magician saws a person in two, but I am sure it is an illusion. (Not least because the magician admits it is an illusion!) It seems to me that philosophers are often criticized for always demanding rational explanations. I think it is fairer to say that philosophers demand either explanations that are rational or none at all. On the whole, philosophers would rather just accept that some things are unexplained than accept a wild explanation just because it's the only one on offer.

A second limitation we have to accept is that our knowledge in such instances is fallible. We could be wrong. It could turn out that the tape is a hoax. We may reject a hundred different conspiracy theories only to discover that one of them is in fact correct. To this we can only say it is unfortunate that this must be so. The idea that knowledge must be in some way infallible is philosophically immature. If we are to understand as best we can what knowledge is, we have to accept the limits on what we can know.

Truth revisited

Earlier I rejected a crude relativism and suggested that we need to accept that there is a difference between what we take to be true and what is true. However, it should be noted that the abductive method is associated with the pragmatist school of philosophy, which does not hold a realist view of knowledge.

Rather, what is true is 'what works'. Put crudely, it is true that petrol is flammable because if you set light to it, it will burn. The atomic theory is true because, if you suppose it to be true, you can do all sorts of things like create nuclear bombs or power stations.

It should be clear that this has nothing to do with crude relativism. It cannot be true for you that petrol burns and not true for me, since what happens when I put a match to petrol is just what happens if you do. 'What works' is independent of us. For this reason, in practice, being a pragmatist is much more like being a realist than a crude relativist. A pragmatist does not think that what we think is true is the same as what is true, since we may think something to be true which 'doesn't work'. This is why the pragmatist, although a non-realist, can argue that the Bin Laden tapes either are or are not genuine.

I mention this point briefly because I think it illustrates how philosophy often 'leaves the world as it is', as Wittgenstein put it. The disagreement between realists and non-realists is about the fundamental nature of truth and falsehood. However, this often does not change how we should talk about truth and falsehood at the level of everyday discourse. When philosophers get together and one of them says that they think the president is telling a lie, for example, they do not usually get into a discussion about what truth is. They might do, but in such a case they are examining the question of what it means to tell a lie, not whether the president actually lied or not. When considering the second question, their discussion is likely to be very similar to that of any other, hopefully intelligent, person.

Conclusion

Bringing together the two threads of this chapter—truth and knowledge—we arrive at a view which is measured and undogmatic, but it isn't an 'anything goes' view. Philosophy should lead, I think, to intellectual modesty. We should be careful not to assert with absolute conviction that we and we alone know the truth. We have to accept that most of what passes for knowledge cannot be proved beyond all doubt. All we can do is reason carefully about what the evidence suggests and reach our conclusions accordingly, always mindful that we could be wrong. Hand in hand with this modesty comes a rejection of false intellectual generosity. Not all points of view are equally 'valid' except in the sense that we all have the right to believe what we will. Simply to claim that truth is in the eye of the beholder is the end of all attempts at intelligent discourse. Similarly, though we may not be able to prove all our beliefs, some are better supported by argument and by experience than others. Philosophy leads us to accept that there are certain standards by which we can judge claims to know the truth, but also that these judgements can never be made with absolute certainty. It is the measured path between absolute dogmatism on the one side and total relativism on the other.

Perhaps the greatest lesson we have learned from philosophers about knowledge is that scepticism is a game which you can't stop people playing if they are determined to do so. Like a court jester, the sceptic can continue to dance and laugh, teasing us with his cries of 'But how can you be sure?' and 'It all might be wrong'. The sceptical jester may have a value in that he may constantly remind us that everything is indeed uncertain. But by always being sceptical, the jester has missed the crucial point—lack of absolute certainty is unavoidable. That's the way the world is. But that is no reason to believe that we can't pursue truth and knowledge. It is simply a reason for us to do so humbly.

It can be sobering to apply these lessons to our reading of current affairs. Something like the war on terrorism is a serious and concerning matter. Some people respond to situations like this by becoming dogmatic and militant. I have not addressed these people directly in this chapter since I would hope that the broad philosophical approach I have set out is, as a whole, a kind of argument against them. I have concerned myself with those who reject dogmatism and replace it with a kind of intellectual despair, a suspension of judgement based on the idea either that there is no truth out there or that we can't know it anyway. The alternative is, I suggest, to accept that there is something we rightly call the truth, even if it is not quite what realists take to be truth, and that our knowledge of this truth is fallible and uncertain. It is harder to struggle to make sense of the news following this path than it is to suspend judgement or dogmatically cling to a fixed viewpoint. But it is, I believe, the only philosophically justifiable way to proceed.

Doing the right thing: Ethics and private life

Sex, drugs, and money

Newspapers love nothing more than exposing a public figure with their trousers down, hands in the till, nose in the powder, or preferably all three. Without sex, drugs, and cash scandals, many popular newspapers would be hard-pressed to fill their pages.

In recent years, one of the most notable examples of the media's hunger for this sort of story is the saga of Bill Clinton and Monica Lewinsky. Tales of the most powerful man in the world, the inventive use to which he put his cigars, and the stained dress Lewinsky conveniently decided not to clean, enthralled, outraged, or bored people the world over.

Drugs provided the fuel for lesser scandals, which came and went. The presenter of a long-running British children's television show was sacked after it was revealed that he had taken cocaine. Members of a pop band with a squeaky-clean image and a massive teen following were forced to make a public apology when it was discovered they had smoked cannabis. Such stories appear in the news with remarkable regularity, their predictability never preventing them from reaching the front pages.

Financial scandals tend to involve politicians and businesspeople rather than celebrities. In Britain, a senior minister, Peter Mandelson, resigned when it came to light that he had accepted a large home loan from a fellow minister, who was himself under investigation by another government department, without disclosing this to several parties who claimed an interest.

Wherever you go in the world, similar stories regularly pepper the news pages. A common reaction is to take such incidents as evidence of the decline in society's moral standards. Such prophecies of moral gloom have also recurred throughout history, and in themselves they are indicative of nothing more than the tendency to see one's own age as degenerate. In our own time, when people talk about the decline of morality, they tend to think of a loosening of standards of sexual conduct, drug-taking, and a move towards individualism.

However, not everyone would agree that these are signs that we are becoming less moral. An alternative view is that we have shifted our view of what the proper subject matter of morality is. What we do with our private lives seems not to matter, as long as it doesn't harm anyone else. The contemporary moral philosopher Peter Singer, for instance, is not alone when he writes, 'sex raises no special moral issues at all'. The real moral issues are those of suffering, lack of liberty, and oppression. What people do with their own time, especially sexually, is their own business.

This disagreement about where the proper focus of morality lies infuses discussion of the case of Bill Clinton. Few people, not even the former president himself, would argue with the fact that Clinton behaved badly. At the very least he betrayed his wife. However, many people think that such affairs of the heart are more part of the ups and downs of life than major moral issues. Blame, responsibility, punishment, and guilt are for the parties involved—and God, if she exists—to sort out. As far as the wider public should be concerned, Clinton's morality in this regard is irrelevant. If he had siphoned off taxes to feather his own nest, that would be a moral issue of public interest. But his sex life is of no concern to anyone but him, his lovers, and his family.

This debate reflects a fundamental difference in thinking on ethics, between those who see the centre of moral gravity in the conduct of our private lives and those who see morality as being centred in the public realm, where our acts affect others. Of course, no one views morality as concerned entirely with private behaviour or entirely with public actions, but, as we shall see, the difference in emphasis is important.

Whichever view is right, what does seem clear is that, having overturned the old moral order, rooted in traditional, religion-based value systems, many people are struggling to find a firm platform from which to make their moral judgements. We talk about such things as rights, responsibilities, justice, freedom, and fairness, but often without a clear conception of what these terms mean. Do we use moral language just to dress up our raw feelings of approval or disapproval, as the British philosopher A. J. Ayer argued back in 1936? Or are there ethical concepts which can be genuinely useful in helping us to resolve moral dilemmas?

Two questions

Untangling these moral issues is a difficult and open-ended task. To help make some progress I shall focus on two questions which tend to get confused when scandals concerning public figures get discussed. First, there is a privacy issue: do the parties involved have a right to have their private affairs kept private or is the public entitled to know about them? Then there is an issue of accountability: do the parties involved have a right to behave as they wish in their personal lives, without that affecting their right to hold office or remain employed?

One might give different answers to these two questions. For instance, one might believe that we have the right to know all about Clinton and Lewinsky, but that we do not have a right to unseat him from public office as a result. You can maintain a right to know about someone's private behaviour while renouncing the right to interfere with his life as a result of what you find out.

I shall set aside the privacy issue until later and begin with the question of what we are permitted to demand of people in the public eye on the basis of information we have about their private lives. The Clinton–Lewinsky story will be taken as a case study. The focus will be specifically on the issues this particular part of the Clinton story raises for the debate over public and private ethics. In particular, it is important to distinguish this discussion from the separate allegations of sexual harassment brought against Clinton and the charges of perjury. From this discussion, some general principles will emerge which will be drawn together at the end of this chapter and applied to the other drugs and money scandals mentioned earlier.

But first we need to remind ourselves of the salient facts about the Clinton–Lewinsky affair.

Shenanigans in the oval office

The Clinton–Lewinsky story has its roots in an investigation into Clinton's involvement in a real estate development known as Whitewater while he was governor of Arkansas. The special prosecutor when this investigation began in January 1994 was Robert B. Fiske Junior. However, in August of that year, Fiske was replaced as special prosecutor by Kenneth Starr. According to many commentators, Starr gunned for Clinton with excessive zeal.

Without Starr leading the investigation, it is possible that the sexual scandal, which also began in 1994, might never have taken on the significance it did. In May 1994, former state clerk Paula Jones filed a sexual harassment suit against Clinton, for acts he was again alleged to have committed while governor of Arkansas. It wasn't until December 1996 that Monica Lewinsky first appeared on the scene, named as a potential witness in Jones's lawsuit.

Not much happened until January 1998, the month when the scandal really began to rock the White House. On 7 January Lewinsky signed an affidavit saying she had not had any sexual relations with Clinton. Five days later, a friend of Lewinsky's, Linda Tripp, handed over tapes of her telephone conversations with Lewinsky to the special prosecutor's office, which provided evidence that Lewinsky had lied under oath and that, by implication, Clinton had also lied.

The crucial development, which followed just four days later, was that Starr was given authority to look into the Lewinsky affair as part of his investigation into the Whitewater deal. The sex and real estate scandals had become enmeshed. Whether this was because of Starr's determination to pursue Clinton or because Clinton's alleged dishonesty was genuinely relevant to the Whitewater inquiry remains a bone of contention.

What happened after this remains etched in the public consciousness. Looking straight into the television cameras, Clinton declared that he 'did not have sexual relations with that woman'.

He also denied telling anybody to lie. The same day, Lewinsky revealed to Tripp that she had a dress with Clinton's semen still on it.

By August, Clinton was forced to change his story. 'I did have a relationship with Miss Lewinsky which was not appropriate,' he again told the nation on television. Starr completed his investigation in September and presented his report claiming it might contain grounds for impeachment. In December Clinton was formally accused of three perjury charges and obstructing justice. After two months of hearings, in which the House of Representatives impeached Clinton on one count of perjury and obstruction of justice, the final arbiters, the Senate, finally acquitted Clinton on 12 February 1999.

The case had dominated the news for months. Yet at the end of it, serious doubts remained as to whether the story should ever have been given the prominence it had. Was this a genuine matter of public concern or just tittle-tattle? Did the president have a right to privacy in his sexual relations? Even if we have a right to know, is this really something he should have been held to public account for?

To clarify the question, it is necessary to deal with one aspect of the case right away. Clinton is alleged to have lied under oath. This is against the law and as such is the proper concern of society. That alone may justify public interest in the affair. But, in a sense, this is not the fundamental issue. Clinton was only put in a position where he may have concealed truths about his private life because he was being called to public account for his sex life. If it was wrong that he should have been called to account for this in the first place, we might consider his subsequent behaviour in a different light. If people did not have a right to know about his sexual antics, was Clinton really so wrong not to answer questions about his private life more directly?

In the discussion that follows, I will put to one side issues concerning lying to the nation and to the courts and focus purely on whether Clinton's affair with Lewinsky was in and of itself a legitimate cause for public concern.

Considering the distinction between the public and the private in ethics will help us to provide some answers. In the Clinton case there is a question about whether his behaviour was moral. But there is also a question about whether it should have any bearing on how we judge him in public life.

Examining this issue may also help us make more sense of ethics in general. Our discussion will consider questions of rights, individual freedom, harm, and conceptions of the good life. By seeing how these questions work themselves out in this particular case, we will be able to draw some general lessons which can help us clarify our moral thinking.

Before going on, however, we need to consider a pair of general distinctions. The first is the difference between ethics and morality, the second between the public and the private. This will help us to have a clearer focus on some of the key issues we need to address.

Morality and ethics

We tend to use the terms 'ethics' and 'morality' interchangeably. However, it can be helpful to make a distinction between them.

Ethics is the study of human conduct—not what people actually do, but what they should do. This 'should' could be of several kinds. According to Kant, the 'should' of ethics is always an absolute or 'categorical' should—we just should do this or that because that's what morality demands. But a 'should' can also be conditional—we should do this or that *if* we want to live our lives to the full, for example. This reading of 'should' is more in line with Aristotle's approach to ethics. It is also possible that an ethical theory will conclude that there are no shoulds—that we are free to do whatever we want.

Morality can be seen as a subset of ethics. A moral code is a set of rules that prescribes how we should act, with the implication that to act otherwise is to do something wrong, perhaps harmful to ourselves or others. Morality thus always has a sense of rules and constraint which ethics need not. In this way, Kant's ethics provides a moral code; Aristotle's does not.

Friedrich Nietzsche argued in his *On the Genealogy of Morals* that morality, in the sense described, is a kind of disfigurement of ethics. Before morality there was a distinction between good and bad, which was the difference between things going well and things going badly. Someone who is destitute leads a bad life in this sense, not because they are doing wrong in the sense of disobeying a moral code but because their life is not going well. Someone prospering, on the other hand, lives a good life, not because they are particularly praiseworthy but because their life is going well.

Christianity, argued Nietzsche, turned this upside down. Those whose lives were going badly reconciled themselves to their fate by calling themselves good and the prosperous whose lives seemed to be good, evil. They thus moralized the idea of the good. Nietzsche thought this was a mistake. Instead of the weak fighting to lead better lives, they chose instead to satisfy themselves with their poor lot, anoint themselves the good, and wait for their reward in the afterlife.

One may disagree with Nietzsche, but the story he tells does give some sense of the distinction between an ethical sense of the good and bad, which is to do with how well life is going, and a more moralistic sense of good and bad or evil, which is to do with breaking moral laws. This distinction is important because too often it is assumed that ethics is just the same as morality, and that therefore ethics is all about rules and prohibitions. We should rid ourselves of that presupposition. What we're considering is how best we should live, and whether or not the answer to that question requires a moral code is something we should not prejudge.

The private/public boundary

A second important distinction is between the public and private ethical spheres. What we include in the private sphere varies. Some regard their private life to involve only themselves while others would include an extended range of friends and family. Wherever one draws the boundary, there is a natural tendency to consider some aspects of our lives as of purely private concern and others of legitimate public interest. In the case of a 'leader of the free world' such as Clinton, the position of this boundary is even more problematic. It can be expected that the president of the United States will, as a matter of course, enjoy less privacy than the average citizen, but how much of his life should he be allowed to keep private?

However, even with ordinary citizens the distinction we make between our private and public lives is not quite as clear-cut as we sometimes like to think it is. Most of what we put under the category of 'private' does directly affect other people outside the private circle. If I take drugs and then drive, I am risking the lives of others as well as my own. If I visit a prostitute, some might argue that I am using another person in a dehumanizing way or helping to maintain the manipulation of vulnerable women by often violent pimps. If I have an affair with a married woman, I cannot deny my part in any disruption that may have to her marriage.

Of course, all these incidents may be given a more positive spin. Drug use may be carried out harmlessly. Some will argue that prostitution may, sometimes, be mutually beneficial to both parties. And an affair with a married person need not always be damaging to other people. My point is not that each of my examples are definitely wrong, but rather that in each case it is not a purely private matter: people outside the sphere of my private life are involved, and if we are to behave well we must consider the effects of our actions on others.

At this point, it may be objected that in each of my examples, apart from the drug use, I don't have to think of others because everyone else directly involved has freely consented to take part. (This assumes, rather dubiously, that parties such as the cuckolded husband are not directly involved.) This is a common reaction, but not, I think, as obviously persuasive as it may first appear. People make their choices based on the options that are available to them at the time. To say a prostitute has freely chosen that life is to ignore all the factors that may have made that 'choice' seem like the only one and the sometimes terrible difficulty of giving it up. If I visited a poor part of the world, I may find desperate families willing to sell me their daughter for, in Western terms, a pittance, in order to secure their basic needs. For me to go ahead with this transaction on the basis that they freely agreed to it would, I think, be appalling. I would be guilty of exploiting their weakness and dressing it up as a freely entered into contract. The moral of this is clear: just because the final decision made seems to be a 'free' one, that doesn't mean that the decision is entirely free and it doesn't absolve me from the responsibility to think of the consequences my choice has for the people affected by it.

There is a second point to be made here too. In the example of the affair, the thought seems to be that I am not responsible for any harm caused to the marriage, as I am not the one involved in the marriage and the person who is involved is thus entirely responsible for any harm done. But again, by analogy to other examples, I think we can treat the justification with some suspicion. Let's say I have a friend who harms her family by gambling away her—the main bread-winner's—money. She is trying to give up gambling, and I want to go to the races. If I were to invite her along, I know she wouldn't be able to resist gambling, she'd probably lose, and her family would have another week with not enough money. Can I turn around and say, 'Well, her family is her responsibility. If she comes with me, it's her choice and I am not responsible for any harm that may come to her family'? I think such a justification would be self-serving and repugnant. Saying that it is all her choice, is deliberately to ignore the harm I know will result. But this is just the kind of justification we use to defend third parties in extramarital affairs. The only significant difference, it seems to me, is that the harm caused by the gambling is much more obvious and inevitable than the harm caused by an affair, which may be non-existent and could even, at times, not be a harm at all, but a benefit. But the principle is the same: we cannot duck our responsibilities by saying that the other party took part freely.

The lesson of all of this is that the realm of the private cannot always easily be divorced from that of the public. So we should be careful before claiming that something is 'purely a private matter'.

Rights and freedom

In the Clinton–Lewinsky case, then, we are not going to be able to come to any quick judgement by a simple distinction between the public and private sphere. Rather, we have to consider whether the public's right to know about the president's behaviour in this case has a stronger claim than the president's right to privacy and freedom to live his own life. To answer this question, we have to consider the nature of rights and freedoms and the extent to which Clinton's 'private' behaviour affects other people.

Look in any political manifesto and the words 'rights' and 'freedom' are sure to feature prominently. Western democracy is arguably built upon the twin pillars of individual freedom and unassailable rights. To be opposed to either is to be opposed to the very basis of democratic society.

It is because freedom and rights are so fundamental that they become dangerous words to use. If someone wants to legitimize what they are doing, even if it is harmful, they will almost certainly try to describe their actions in terms of freedom and rights. People defend such controversial practices as tobacco manufacture and sale, hunting animals for sport, and pornography on the grounds that we are free people who have the right to enjoy whatever pleasures we choose. Whatever the merits of these arguments, we should be careful of taking them at face value. Historically, people have argued for the right to own slaves, to pay people inadequate wages, or to throw people off land they have worked and lived on all their lives. The language of rights and freedom can be used to disguise all kinds of injustices and wrongdoings.

We therefore have reason to be wary of the defence which says that, since it is a free country, Clinton can have as many consensual affairs with interns as he wants and can get. People have the right to personal freedom and that means we have no right to pull them over the coals for behaving in private in ways of which we don't approve. The argument sounds persuasive, but as I have already said, arguments that appeal to rights and freedom often do, just because we are all in favour of rights and freedom. But in order to think philosophically about anything, you have to look beyond what sounds persuasive. The way something sounds may not be how it actually is revealed to be on closer inspection. And the fact that something is persuasive may not mean that it is well argued or justified.

The idea of freedom is closely associated with that of rights: to say I am free to do something is to say I have the right to do that thing free from interference. Rights are generally considered to be fundamental and unassailable. But they are not trump cards. Rights sometimes conflict, and in such cases, we need to decide which right is more important and should take precedence. I have a right to free speech, for example, and others have a right to go about their business unhindered. If I follow someone around exercising my right to free speech by shouting at the top of my voice that this person is a child molester, when that is untrue, my right to free speech is in conflict with this person's right to non-interference. In this case, I hope most of us would agree that it is my right which is defeated and thus it would be justifiable for my free speech to be curtailed.

One can quite readily imagine more conflicts of rights. Rights of private property can clash with rights of free movement, as the recent debate in England and Wales over the 'right to roam' in the countryside has shown. The right to remain silent can conflict with the right to justice. The right to freedom can be denied to protect the rights of others to live without fear. So one question we must ask of all the cases under consideration is whether the rights of the individuals concerned are in conflict with the rights of anyone else.

What is interesting here is that people will invoke all sorts of rights to support their stance. Consider the person who takes an anti-Clinton line and wants to insist that his affairs are not just private matters but of public concern. You can hear such people appealing to all sorts of rights, such as the right to have a president with the dignity the office demands. The problem is that defenders of Clinton can appeal to a conflicting right: the right for people in the public eye to have a private life free from public scrutiny.

This is why appeals to rights are in themselves inconclusive. In the debate over abortion, we have an appeal to the baby's right to life on the one hand, and an appeal to the mother's right to choose on the other. In business, we have appeals to the rights of workers to strike pitted against the rights of employers to hire whom they want. In immigration we have the rights of individuals to live where they want conflicting with the rights of governments to decide who enters and lives within their borders.

The invoking of a right, therefore, is not the end of the matter. It is merely the beginning. What we really need to do is see whose right is the strongest. Is your right to have a dignified president who is honest in his private life more important than the president's right for a personal life that remains private?

The bases for rights

To answer these questions we need to look at what the bases for these rights are, or, indeed, whether they are genuine rights at all. We often talk about rights as though they were just there, part of our natural inheritance. Many philosophers, however, have followed Jeremy Bentham in saying that such talk of natural rights is 'nonsense upon stilts'. This scepticism about rights is infectious once one starts to question the nature and basis of many of the rights which are claimed.

For instance, is there really a right to have a president with an appropriate dignity? Where could such a right have come from? How would you even set about defining what amount and kind of dignity the right demands? If we start granting rights such as these, what other 'rights' would we have to acknowledge? Do we have a right to expect anyone who holds public office or is in the public eye to behave well at all times, even in private? The suggestion is surely absurd and debases the very notion of a right. Calls for human rights to be upheld lose some of their urgency if human rights cover apparently trivial matters such as the dignity of our leaders, rather than fundamental issues of life, liberty, and freedom. Just as if you print too much money, its value goes down, so if you grant too many rights, the moral significance of a right becomes debased. We should bear that in mind before we try to claim anything as a right.

Ideally, to settle any dispute about rights, we would have a general procedure for determining which right is genuine, or which right is paramount. To do this we would need a complete theory of rights. However, it is a mistake to suppose that progress in applied philosophy can only be made if we first get a complete general theory in place. We can usually learn a great deal just by thinking clearly about the case in question. In this case, what is at issue is whether the public has a right to insist on certain standards of behaviour from people in public office or whether such people have a right to lead their private lives as they themselves see fit.

Given that one would ordinarily grant someone the right to their privacy, the burden of proof in this instance appears to lie on those who would claim Clinton's right to privacy is overridden in this instance. There are three major arguments that could be given to justify this. One is that the right to privacy can be overridden by the need to serve the greater public good. This argument effectively says that Clinton's behaviour lies on the public side of the boundary between the public and the private. A second argument is that one's right to privacy can be overridden for a person's own good. The third is that someone loses the right to privacy if what they do in private is wrong. Consider each in reverse order.

Wrong is wrong

Some would argue that Clinton should have been impeached just because what he did was wrong. In a just world, wrongdoing can't go unpunished.

How should one respond to an argument like this? If you disagree with the argument, it may seem that the best way to go on the offensive is to deny that Clinton committed any actual wrongdoing. But that would be to hack off the branches of the argument rather than to undermine the roots. If you do show that Clinton did no wrong, you haven't actually shown the basic principle of the argument is wrong, merely that it doesn't apply in this instance. Furthermore, in this particular case, it seems evident that Clinton did do something wrong. So the core of the issue is not whether he is blameless, but whether this justifies public censure or punishment.

The most effective way of dealing with the argument is to tackle the underlying principle head on: that all wrongdoing should be punished. Perhaps surprisingly—for expressed like that it seems unobjectionable—this principle is weak. What it amounts to—unless we think we can leave it to God or vigilantes to deal out the punishment—is the idea of 'moral legalism', that one should outlaw all wrongdoing. But do we really want all wrongdoing to be illegal? Imagine if you could be arrested for telling lies, being unfaithful to your partner, making people miserable by your inconsiderate manner, and so on. We do lots of wrong things every day, but to suppose that all such wrongdoings should be illegal is surely to grant too much to the law.

I shall assume that few would want to argue for this kind of extreme moral legalism (although some people who argue that state law should effectively embody religious law perhaps do take this hard line). Most of us would accept that the law should only apply to certain kinds of wrongdoing. This reveals something important about the relationship between law and morality. Although we all want laws which are moral, the legal and the moral are not the same thing: they are not 'coextensive domains'. The law should be based in morality, but is not the same thing as morality. To put it another way, no law should be immoral, but not all of morality should be enforced by law. Without this distinction, we are back to legal moralism.

This introduces a complexity into the Clinton case. We may come to different conclusions about whether Clinton did wrong when he had an affair with Lewinsky. Indeed, there is plenty of evidence that he did do wrong. He lied to his wife and possibly exploited his position of authority over a young intern. But as soon as we start demanding that people resign or be sacked for any wrong action, we are moving from a purely moral judgement to a legal one: we are saying that this is a kind of immorality which should either be punished by law, or the law should allow employers to punish.

We don't think that the law should permit people to be sacked for committing just any kind of wrongdoing. If you were sacked for lying to your spouse you would rightly claim unfair dismissal, since such a wrongdoing is unrelated to your ability and fitness to do your job. So the question we need to answer is this: when should the law punish, or permit others to punish, a person who does something morally wrong? The most plausible answer is when the wrongdoings cause significant and relevant harm. The word 'significant' is indispensable here, for many of the everyday wrongdoings I have listed harm people, but we would not consider it appropriate to seek the law's protection from these harms.

Relevance is also essential, since it would again seem unfair to sack someone for, say, reckless driving if their job is antiques restoration. However, it might be appropriate if they are a travelling salesman and the ability to drive safely is a prerequisite for the job.

It should also be noted that having an affair with a junior colleague is not usually considered a dismissible offence. We often disapprove of such behaviour, but unless there is sexual harassment, from a legal point of view there is no basis for punitive action.

In the Clinton case this should lead us to reject the argument that the affair with Lewinsky was a legitimate concern of the state prosecutor simply because it was wrong. For it to be of public interest, the wrongdoing must cause harm which is both relevant and significant. This then collapses into the justification that Clinton forfeits his right to privacy because his actions harmed others, which we will turn to shortly. Before that, we need to consider whether we would be justified in bringing Clinton to account for his own good.

For our own good

Is society justified in punishing individuals for their own good, even when they have not harmed others? In the case we are considering, this seems to be a red herring, because no one claims that Clinton should have been impeached for his own good. So the 'for your own good' argument in this case doesn't get off the ground.

In any case, the idea that the law should protect us from ourselves, or 'legal paternalism' as it is termed, is not one which enjoys more than qualified support. There are a few examples of what seems to be legal paternalism in the UK—compulsory wearing of seat belts and the banning of certain drugs are two examples. But such laws only gain support because the harms they are preventing are very serious indeed and the restrictions they place upon us not onerous. Indeed, in the case of certain drugs, the argument that the harms caused are not so great and the restrictions unduly limiting on lifestyle choices have made the prohibitive laws controversial and widely ignored. Furthermore, in these cases the laws are not justified solely by legal paternalism. Drug use is restricted partly because drug users and dealers are alleged to harm others. One consequence of people not using seat belts is that when vehicles crash there are more strains on the emergency services and back-seat passengers can kill those in the front seat.

Legal paternalism, therefore, is not much use to the person who wishes to justify the calls for public figures to resign, be sacked, or apologize for supposed wrongdoings in their private lives. That leads us to the final possible justification for such demands: the harms their actions have for society.

Harming others

Although much can be done by using the tools of philosophical thinking without consulting the great works in the philosophical literature, sometimes we can gain important insight by listening to what the greats had to say. In this case, we can be helped considerably by looking at John Stuart Mill's 'harm principle':

The only purpose for which power can rightfully be exercised over any member of a civilised community, against his will, is to prevent harm to others. His own good, either physical or moral, is not a sufficient warrant.

The harm principle rules out legal paternalism, which we have already dealt with. But it does provide a justification for preventing actions which harm others. The question is, when Clinton has oral sex with an intern, a politician fails to declare loans made by colleagues, or pop singers smoke cannabis, are they harming anyone else?

Mill helps us to answer this question by distinguishing between harm and offence. Mill thought that one is not justified in preventing someone from doing something or punishing them for doing it merely because we are offended by it. The reason for this should be pretty obvious: too many people are offended by too many different things to make this practical. Some people may be offended by the knowledge that others practise anal sex; some by the fact that others eat meat; some by the fact that others pray to Jesus rather than Allah, or vice versa. We just can't include such offence in our concept of harm. We might want to limit what people can do in public because of the offence it causes, but since all the cases we are looking at are of private behaviour, this doesn't help us here.

So the question we need to answer is whether Clinton's actions harmed other people sufficiently to justify being held to public account. Clinton harmed his own family by his actions, but this kind of emotional harm to those we have close relationships with is not the business of public morality or the law. (Remember we are only concerned here with whether the affair was of legitimate public concern. We are setting aside issue such as Clinton's lying under oath.) As we have seen, not everything that is wrong should be punished by law or be allowed to be punished within the law. So there does not seem to be any harm caused by the Clinton–Lewinsky affair which would take it out of the purely private domain and justify a public interest.

Back to rights and freedom

Our discussion has tried to provide some answers to fundamental questions about rights and freedoms. At issue is whether people in public life have a right to go about their own private lives without what they do in those lives affecting decisions about their suitability to continue in their public roles. Nothing in what we have considered so far shows that right should be taken away. No one has a right to take away our employment or position of public office just because we have done something wrong in our private lives. Nor can they do so just because what we are doing is not the best thing for ourselves. And in sexual relations, offence may be caused to others not involved in the relations, but only if actual harm were caused could it justify punishment. Our rights to do what we want cannot be taken away just because what we do offends some people.

However, in philosophy one has to be very careful before one draws general conclusions from specific arguments. The evidence we have considered so far may support public figures' rights for their private behaviour not to affect their public appointments, but maybe other arguments and other evidence would provide sufficient support for a different conclusion. If a conclusion is not supported by an argument, that means only that support for a conclusion is lacking, not necessarily that the conclusion is wrong. It gives us reason not to advance the conclusion, but not definitively to decide it is wrong. In this case, no 'killer' argument has been advanced which shows that the private lives of celebrities and politicians do not impinge on their fitness for public life. We have merely failed to find any reasons that show that in general they must.

Is ethics unconcerned with private behaviour?

One may get the feeling there is something lacking in the account so far. Knowing what we do about the way Clinton behaves does change what many of us think about his fitness for office. The way he acts in his sex life seems to inform how we view his public role. Yet the arguments so far seem to say we are wrong to make such a connection.

We might come to a different conclusion if we approach the issues from another angle. From what we have seen so far, it would seem that our private lives are pretty unimportant in ethics. Only when we harm others do ethical issues arise at all, let alone the possibility that this permits legal interference. Is this right?

To answer this we have to return to my earlier remarks about ethics. Ethics is about what is appropriate conduct and not just about right and wrong in the finger-wagging moral sense. When the ancient Greeks talked about ethics, they were interested in how to live the good life, by which they meant a life which is a good one for me, not a life in which I don't break certain rules. Most of them agreed that living the good life involved behaving morally in ways we would recognize: not exploiting others, keeping our word, and so on. But when you realize that Aristotle also talked about how many friends one should have in his master work, the *Nicomachean Ethics*, you get some sense of how differently they viewed the subject.

So if we broaden out ethics in this way and look at what the right way to live for me is, does that affect how we view our private lives? I think it must, because when we judge how well our lives are going we tend to look most closely at precisely those things that concern our private lives: our relationships, lifestyle, personal wealth, and happiness. So clearly our private lives are the subject of ethics, understood as the study of how we can live life better.

This way of thinking about ethics requires a kind of mental reorientation. Consider first what is perhaps now the normal way of looking at the right and wrong of certain actions. If we reflect at all on the morality of our actions, we tend to run through a kind of calculation of benefits and harms, and as long as the benefits outweigh the harms, we feel morally justified. This way of thinking follows in the consequentialist tradition, and is in particular indebted to the utilitarianism of Jeremy Bentham and John Stuart Mill. Their 'greatest happiness principle' stated that morally right actions are those that increase happiness and diminish pain for the greatest number; morally wrong ones are those that diminish happiness and increase pain.

What if Bill Clinton fell for his intern and applied these principles? Let us suppose what turned out not to be true, that he could have expected to have conducted this affair in secret. He had a 'moral' choice to make. Does he 'have sexual relations' with this young woman he finds sexually attractive and who wants sexual relations with him?

How does the moral calculation work out in this case? Well, we have the intense pleasure of the sex on the positive side, and on the negative side, the small chance that the intern is psychotic and the usual controllable risks of sexually transmissible disease and/or pregnancy. In other words, Clinton could have weighed some pretty sure-thing pluses on the one hand against some small chances of bad things on the other, with no obvious harm caused to anyone else. If he thought things through on that basis, it would have been no surprise that he took the sex.

Had Clinton reasoned in this way, he would have missed some other considerations which may have altered his view somewhat. The reason for this is that the basis of such decision-making is very limited, being based only on the direct and immediate benefits and harms of his actions. But if we are interested in our lives going well, we should not just concern ourselves with such immediate results, we should also think about the bigger picture. This is something any sophisticated utilitarian would do.

An important part of this bigger picture, which Aristotle recognized over two millennia ago, is character. He thought we became good or bad people (remember these are not strictly moral senses of the words) by what habits and aspects of character we cultivated. To take one not particularly Aristotelian example, if we want to be able to enjoy trusting, open relationships, we have to cultivate a trusting, open character. (Which is not the same as being naive or innocent.) If we consistently behave in a way which discourages these character traits, we run the risk of not being able to enjoy the trusting, open relationships we seek. People are different, and so generalizations are hard, but it is certainly possible for at least some people who choose regularly to enjoy opportunistic sex, that by doing so they cultivate certain aspects of their character that may not be conducive to these trusting, open relationships. These may include: treating people as mere sex objects; concealing one's feelings to avoid a casual affair getting complicated; developing the tendency to act opportunistically rather than consistently; becoming unable to treat sexual partners as intimate friends; viewing one's own self-esteem in terms of who we can attract. None of these is the inevitable result of habitual causal sex, but nonetheless they are all possible and arguably not uncommon consequences.

My main point is not that the specific consequences I suggest might follow do actually follow, it is rather the more general point that how we behave contributes to who we become, and that, importantly, this is a consequence that is not apparent when we simply list the pros and cons of individual actions. When we are thinking about the ethics of the way we live our lives, therefore, I think there is far more to it than often appears. We very rarely harm others directly, and we tend to think of morality in terms of harms and benefits to others. But ethics is more general than this. It is about the effects our actions have on the people we become as well as the more indirect effects of what we do on others. Easier though it is to ignore these things than to accept them, if we are to get the most out of life and live in a way which we can respect, we must take these things into account.

Character and public life

In some respects, recognizing the ethical importance of character changes nothing. The arguments up to this point have supported the conclusion that we are only justified in seeking redress from people in public life for their wrongdoing if their actions harm others. The fact that the way we act reflects and moulds our character, and thus should not be considered in pure isolation, doesn't change this. It may, however, justify a public interest in knowing about these character flaws. Remember how earlier I distinguished between two issues. First, there was the privacy issue: do people in public life have a right to have their private affairs kept private or is the public entitled to know about them? Second, there was the issue of accountability: do people in public life have a right to behave as they wish in their private lives, without that affecting their right to hold office or remain employed?

As concerns the second issue, it may seem that nothing I have said about character changes anything. We cannot demand that people are fired or resign on the basis of their 'bad character'. For a start, who would decide what indicates a bad character? It may be true that a person's dishonesty in their romantic life reflects the broader dishonesty of their character in general, but we cannot presume this is the case or set ourselves up as people most competent to judge. In a free society, people are and should only be punished for bad behaviour which causes significant harm to others. The minute we start punishing them for their character we start operating as 'thought police', with all the negative, Orwellian connotations that phrase implies.

However, for certain public offices, character may be decisive. If a priest, for example, is found to be dishonest, that is surely relevant to any judgement which is made about his fitness for office. Judges are in a similar position.

Having said that, I am unconvinced that Clinton's sexual behaviour does make him less fit for office. Indeed, one could argue that it is desirable that politicians can be duplicitous. One just can't be effective in politics unless one is at least a little disingenuous. The virtues of character we most admire in ordinary people may unfortunately hinder people in politics, a point the philosopher Bernard Williams has examined in more detail in his book *Moral Luck*.

But what about the first issue, that of privacy? If the way we behave reflects and moulds our characters and it is wrong to think of morality as being just about the harms of specific actions, isn't there a public interest in knowing about the wrongdoing of people in public life?

The argument that character is important to ethics was often used in Bill Clinton's case, although more often than not it was used not only to try to justify public interest, but also to try to justify impeachment. The latter I believe was unsuccessful as a justification, since I have argued that this kind of character flaw does not show he is unsuitable for the office of president. But in the case of justifying public interest the argument carried more weight. We elect people to hold office because we believe they are up to the job and it is not unreasonable to suppose that judgements we make about their characters are important in deciding whether they are or not. Knowing that a politician is duplicitous in his private life may therefore be relevant to how we judge his character as a whole, and as we have a right to use character as part of the criteria for electing politicians, we are arguably entitled to information which sheds light on his character. However, I personally remain unconvinced that this is a sufficient reason to justify public interest in the Clinton case. Sexual infidelity is just too common a feature of human behaviour for it to reveal anything about a person's suitability for public office. Too many effective leaders have behaved badly in their love lives to make credible the claim that being a 'love rat' is incompatible with being a good president.

General principles

The media takes a great interest in the private lives of famous people and it often picks up on their failings and calls for them to resign, be sacked, or issue public apologies because of them. They are in this sense the self-appointed moral guardians of society. But are they justified in doing this?

My own judgement is that for the most part they are not. Where politicians are involved, unless they are causing serious harm to others, at most we are entitled to take an interest and know about aspects of their private life which cast significant light on those parts of their character relevant to their fitness for public office. But this doesn't mean we are entitled to know about all their peccadilloes. In particular, whom they sleep with is of no concern to the electorate. Bill Clinton's behaviour may have been ethically dubious for several reasons. He may well have harmed people close to him and his behaviour may have contributed to making him a worse character than he might otherwise have been. But none of these are reasons for the public to demand impeachment or sacking. The Clinton case was of greater public concern only because of issues of concealment under oath and obstructing justice, which were directly relevant to his fitness for office. Yet such punishable offences may never have arisen if his private life had not become a matter of public interest in the first place.

How do these principles relate to the other stories I mentioned at the start of the chapter? Consider the case of the drug-taking celebrities first. Matters are complicated because illegal drugs were involved. If one is caught and charged or cautioned, this is a matter of public record and therefore one has already forfeited one's right to privacy. But more often than not, such exposés of celebrity behaviour do not focus on illegal acts, but stories of 'love rats' and getting drunk. To call for public apologies or record companies to pull out of contracts in these circumstances is not justified when no serious harm has been done to others. And since the characters of pop stars are not relevant to their ability to perform good music, there is no public right even to know about such behaviour.

Considering the case from the perspective of the character issue does not change matters. Being of upright character is not at all a prerequisite for being a pop star. The moral integrity of a performer is irrelevant to their artistic output. If their records are themselves immoral (whatever that might mean) that is another issue. But how they behave in private is a separate matter and of no legitimate concern to anyone else.

Some might argue that, as their fans are generally very young, such performers need to 'set an example'. This might be true, but surely only for their behaviour in public. Pop stars set a bad example if they do wrong while performing or making a public appearance, but not if they do wrong in their private lives. The press cannot use this to justify dragging the bad behaviour into the public realm, for if they had left it where it was, no bad example could possibly have been set.

In the Mandelson case, both public interests and calls for

resignation are more clearly justified, since it is part of the rules of being an elected politician that one declares one's financial interests. This is important because we need to know that politicians are not in anyone's debt and could as a consequence be swayed by pressure from them. Here there was an issue of trust and confidence. We need to know that our politicians are honest and open in their political dealings, and are not acting to do favours to their friends. Whether they are honest and open in their romantic lives is another issue. Arguably, Mandelson's secret loan undermined this confidence, both in him as an individual and in politicians as a group. His concealment was about his financial obligations and debt to a person also in politics, who could therefore have some leverage. This is not merely a matter of causing offence, but of seriously damaging the values of trust and openness on which politics depends. Of the three cases under consideration, this is the only one where a clear case of harm to others justifying public calls for remedial actions can be made.

Conclusion

I have set out my own conclusions above. But my main concern is not to win converts to my views but rather to lay bare some of the philosophical issues and arguments that lie behind news stories such as these. Several have emerged during the discussion. Perhaps the most general is the issue of how far we are justified in placing limits on people's private behaviour, either by making that behaviour public or by punishing them for it. Do we believe legal moralism is the answer—making illegal anything we consider morally wrong? Or do we think that we only have a right to intervene when harm to others is involved? If so, how serious need the harm be, given that it must be more than mere offence?

The discussion has also raised issues concerning two different approaches to ethics. One approach focuses on the consequences of individual actions, the other on how individual actions and character are linked. If we believe character is ethically important, that might justify an interest in some aspects of the private lives of public officials, such as politicians. But perhaps more importantly, it informs how we think more generally about ethics and ourselves. It suggests that seeing ethics as merely about the morality of actions, as they affect others, is impoverished and limiting. It enables us to see ethics as broader, richer, and more relevant than it sometimes seems.

Thinking in this way offers us a way back into ethics. Many people find it hard to think about ethics without the moral certainties of religious commandments. What our discussion has shown is that one can do a great deal of thinking about ethics without a religious, command-based belief system. Even if God is dead, ethics lives on.

—

3

Bush vows to use good times for great goals

From Ben Macintyre
in Philadelphia

GEORGE W. BUSH was preparing to accept the Republican presidential nomination last night with a speech designed to change himself as a political moderate ... to one

is the time for Republicans and Democrats to end the politics of fear and save social security, together."

A day after Richard Cheney, Mr Bush's running-mate, lambasted the Democratic Administration, the candidate's words struck a gentler note, but still observed of the Clinton White House, more in sorrow than in anger: "So much promise, to no great purpose." Mr Bush enjoys a showed that after the over his

opponent, Vice-President Al Gore, with one poll putting the gap at 14 points.

Mr Bush's address included a call to improve public schools, strengthen social security, modernise medical care for the elderly, strengthen the Armed Forces and cut taxes.

Mr Cheney sent Republican spirits soaring ahead of Mr Bush's speech with a stinging declaration of war against the Clinton-Gore Administration. "It is time for them to go". Casting aside the non-com-

bative rhetoric that has characterised the Republican convention, the former Defence Secretary launched a withering partisan attack on Mr Gore, painting the Democratic candidate as a mean-minded bully offering only "a thousand attacks".

"We are all a little weary of the Clinton-Gore routine," Mr Cheney declared before a jubilant, confetti-covered crowd on Wednesday night after the Texas Governor was formally nominated as the party's candidate. "Bill Clinton vowed not long ago to hold on to power until the last hour of the last day ... But my friends, that last hour is coming. That last day is near. The wheel has turned and it is time — it is time for them to go."

Describing Mr Bush as "a man of principle who will restore ... energy and integrity to ... Mr Cheney went on ... Mr Gore to ... Clinton

ICAN DREAM

Ballot bores: Rethinking politics

Omnipresent politics

Politics is not just another theme in the news. To a great extent, it is the news. Politics dominates the news bulletins and newspapers like nothing else. Only in times of tragedy and war (which in any case has been said by Carl von Clausewitz to be a continuation of politics by other means) does politics get seriously marginalized in the news, and even then coverage does not stop.

For that reason, I do not wish to single out one example of a political news story for the focus of discussion in this chapter. The point about politics in the news, and our thinking about it, is that it is thinly and widely spread. We need to consider our general reactions and thinking about politics to be able to make better sense of specific news stories. We have to look up from our absorption in the political news story of the day and understand the bigger picture.

To do this I'm going to consider some of the recurring criticisms which were made of the British new Labour government in its first term of 1997–2001. From its name to its policies, new Labour was very strongly influenced by the new Democrats in the United States, so much of what is said here will find echoes in recent US political history. Like the Democrats, Labour had found itself out of power much more often than in. Like America, in the 1980s Britain had re-elected a neo-liberal, right-wing leader and the left seemed to be out of touch with the general mood of the nation. Both Labour and the Democrats found themselves wondering if they'd ever return to power.

The solution for both parties was a radical reinvention and an attempt to ditch their old-style 'tax and spend' and 'big government' images and try to broaden their appeal from the ever-shrinking traditional working classes to middle America and middle Britain. In both cases, these changes resulted in success. Bill Clinton was elected twice as president—the first time the Democrats have held the White House for two successive terms since the 1960s—while new Labour won two elections in a row by landslides—delivering the first two full terms of Labour government in history.

But despite its success, new Labour has been the subject of cynicism and criticism. Many 'old Labour' supporters have said that new Labour is not real Labour at all. They claim Labour has abandoned the socialist aspiration for an equal society and that it has become a purely pragmatic electoral machine, which lacks values. From the right as well as from its own more liberal wing, new Labour has been accused of being overly paternalistic and intrusive, increasingly demanding of citizens that they fulfil their responsibilities—as defined by the government—in order to remain entitled to their rights.

These criticisms infuse the political coverage of newspapers, if not the television. British newspapers are extremely partisan. Although almost all British newspapers eventually came out to support new Labour come election time, in the long years in between the party came in for plenty of the kind of criticism I have sketched. A lot of it comes from newspapers traditionally supportive of Labour, such as the *Guardian*. In order to judge whether these criticisms are fair, we of course need to know what the details of particular policies are. But we also need to get a firm grip on the terms of the debate, such as equality, freedom, and rights. It is this philosophical work which we're going to look at here.

Politics and political philosophy

Before we begin, it is worth saying a few words about the general relationship between political philosophy and politics. The British prime minister, Tony Blair, was widely ridiculed in February 2002 when he was unable to provide 'a brief characterisation of the political philosophy which he espouses and which underlies his policies' when asked to do so in Parliament by a member of his own party (who was also a former university lecturer in philosophy). But perhaps the ridicule was unfair, since the connection between politics and political philosophy is not quite as strong or direct as one might expect. The British political philosopher Jonathan Wolff has said, for example, 'Political philosophers shouldn't, I think, be trying to create policy. They don't know how to.' Wolff's reason for saying this is that political philosophy is concerned with general questions of principle and theory, not with implementation. A philosopher might be able to say which principles a political programme should be following, but she may be unable to say which actual policies are best able to deliver on these principles.

More broadly, the point is that political philosophy is only one part of politics. Politics is not just about having a clear philosophy, it is also about knowing the facts, understanding how the economy works, being able to respond to voter demand, diplomacy, crisis management, pragmatism, compromise, and conflict. In short, a politician is not and cannot be someone who needs only follow certain principles of political philosophy. She must 'get her hands dirty' because politics in the real world is not just about philosophy and principles. Anyone going into politics who thinks otherwise is destined for a short career, not because politics is so corrupt that such people cannot survive in it, but because politics is a practical, not a theoretical enterprise.

Similar considerations apply when thinking about oneself as a voter or political agent. While I believe it can be extremely helpful to bring philosophical considerations to bear on our interpretation and understanding of politics, philosophy alone cannot tell us how to act. Perhaps the most striking example here is thinking about whether it is worth voting at all. Many decision theorists would say it is not: the vote of an individual is insignificant in all but the most marginal of elections. If you want a certain party to win, it is better that you persuade many others to vote for them than vote yourself. Furthermore, depending on the electoral system, it can be ineffectual to vote for the party you support anyway. This is a particular problem in the United Kingdom, where votes take place in constituencies of on average 68,000 people and the candidate with the most votes wins. Many such constituencies are 'safe seats' where the same party regularly wins with an unassailable majority. Even when the seat is not safe, it is usually the case that only two of the candidates stand a realistic chance of winning. In such instances, the practicalities of the voting system and the facts concerning the popularity of candidates are arguably much more important factors in one's voting choice than philosophical considerations.

As with much else, then, it is important to recognize that there is much more to say about politics than can be said by a philosopher. As I repeatedly argue in this book, philosophy can help illuminate our understanding of current affairs but it cannot do the job alone.

Blurred vision

There is an image of the philosopher as a kind of intellectual fireman, who may be called in to quell blazing rows that are the result of muddled thinking or sloppy argument. While it would be arrogant to suppose that this intellectual fire brigade comprises only philosophers, there is some truth in the idea that a good dose of philosophy can often be of help whenever thoughts get tangled.

In politics, our intellectual vision can be blurred because our beliefs and allegiances often have strong emotive elements. Since Plato, many philosophers have sought to make a sharp distinction between reason and emotion. Increasingly, the extent of the division is being questioned. Nevertheless, all can agree that clear thinking is much more difficult when our passions rule, and politics can arouse great passions. Just think, for example, about how a lot of people view those whose political allegiances differ from their own. They often think that such people are flawed in some way and that they could never vote for them, even if, as a matter of fact, they do change their allegiances in the long run.

These emotional ties should not be underestimated. I know one very intelligent person who was a lifelong Labour party member (though barely middle-aged) but who at the last election thought that the Liberal Democrats had a significantly better set of policies. What is more, he actively disliked the direction new Labour was heading. Did he then vote Liberal Democrat? No. Party allegiance meant he both campaigned for and voted for new Labour. I can see why he did so but cannot for the life of me see how such allegiance can be seen as a good thing.

Emotional attachment can also work in another way. Many people become attached to a particular ideology, such as that of old Labour. Although that ideology was challenged and rejected by the party as a whole, many within it and its supporters continue to hold on to it. There is nothing wrong with this, as long as the old ideology is being maintained because there are still good reasons to think it is right. But in too many cases it seems that the attachment people have to old Labour is a purely emotional one. Old certainties aren't held on to because they are true but because they are reassuring.

That is not to say that emotion has no place in politics. Far from it. If one is convinced that the country is being run badly and that people are suffering as a result, then an emotional reaction is not only acceptable, but, I would have thought, desirable. However, if we can never put our feelings to one side, we will simply persist in our convictions even if the facts have changed or the sophistication of our reasoning has improved.

It is even more important to put aside hatred of individuals or groups. In the UK, for example, it is remarkable how vitriolic views of members of other parties can become. Many on the left view Conservatives as nasty, greedy, and hypocritical to a man. Others on the right view socialists as losers, hypocrites, or naive idealists. This is one of the rare occasions when we can learn from the politicians themselves, who often show much more respect and friendship towards their political adversaries than the voters do. One former Member of Parliament told me the only real friends he made there were with people from other parties. Our problem is that if we identify political ideas too closely with people we take to be nasty or stupid, it becomes virtually impossible to take a measured view of the political ideas themselves. 'It must be bad or wrong because X believes it' is a logical nonsense—Hitler was a vegetarian, but anyone who thinks that shows vegetarianism is wrong has just lazily applied the fallacious principle of guilt by association. Not everything our opponents believe is false, so although it may be revealing to see who supports a particular policy or party, such considerations alone will not tell us if it is correct or not.

Along with passion, the other great enemy of rational thought in politics is habit. In the most extreme cases, this is where people support a particular political party simply because that's what they've always done. Obviously, anyone who values thinking at all will need no persuading that this is not a good basis for political allegiance. Slightly less extreme are those people who always support the same party, but when asked why they do, come up with reasons which seem to have been taken on years ago and not examined since. For example, prior to the 1997 general election in the United Kingdom, many opinion polls gauged the opinions of voters on the two main political parties, the right-wing Conservatives and the left-wing Labour party. Many people, often a majority, agreed with statements such as, 'There's always high inflation under Labour', 'We pay less tax under the Conservatives', 'The Tories cut spending on the NHS', and 'Labour are against privatization'. All of these are factually inaccurate. In the last case, by the next general election many were actually criticizing the Labour government for being obsessed with privatization. In these examples, it could be said that facts, rather than philosophy, are what is lacking. This is partly true. But it is also the case that philosophy is an activity which encourages rational scrutiny and questioning. People who have incorrect beliefs about politics may be making factual, not philosophical errors, but their failure to subject these beliefs to scrutiny is philosophical, not factual.

All these reasons together show why the debate about whether new Labour is real Labour is largely sterile. We need to transcend the emotional attachments or antipathies we may have towards political parties and examine them for what they are now. We need to make sure our support or disapproval is not granted by habit but because it is merited. To do this we need to consider whether new Labour or the new Democrats meet the needs of today, not whether they resemble the Labour or Democrats of yesterday.

The role of principles

One criticism of new Labour is that it has betrayed its principles. The accusation is serious because our thinking about politics is often, though not necessarily always, led by certain core principles or values we hold. Most Labour supporters in the UK, like Democrats in the USA, count among these principles a commitment to a more equal society and a particular concern to put the interests of the poorest and weakest above those of the most wealthy. Critics say that with, for example, the commitment in Labour's first term not to increase the highest rates of income tax, these principles have been betrayed.

Although principles alone are not enough for a full and effective political programme, they are arguably indispensable. But what follows from an adherence to such principles is often far from obvious. The fact that we hold a particular principle does not tell us what we should do to uphold it, nor whether other principles need to be put first. For example, we may ask whether we think that the principles we believe in must be upheld at all cost. In some cases, we might find that we believe they do. A committed pacifist, for example, believes that we should never go to war whatever the circumstances, even if our own annihilation would surely follow. But such inflexible principles are rare, because most of us can recognize at least some conceivable circumstances where some principles need to be compromised in order to safeguard other important ones. Most traditional Labour supporters, for example, believe in greater equality of income, but they wouldn't want this to be achieved at the price of a lower quality of life for all. Some inequality would be a fair price to pay for a society where there is no absolute poverty and little relative poverty. The political philosopher John Rawls has formalized this in his difference principle, which states that inequality is acceptable only to the extent that the worst off in society are better off with this inequality than they would be without it. (I will look more closely at the issue of equality later in this chapter.) Such a principle could justify the taxation policies which some attack as a betrayal of equality. For various reasons best explained by an economist, punitive taxes for high earners can actually result in a decreased tax take and can also decrease economic growth. This can mean fewer jobs and less money available for the government to help those worst off. Thus it could be the case that taking the step which seems most likely to increase equality—taxing the rich heavily—is actually in the worst interests of the very people supporters of greater equality want to help. I'm not saying this is the case, only that it could be the case, and this very possibility shows that making the link between principles and policy is not straightforward.

Perhaps the most important consideration about principles concerns the distinction between means and ends. This distinction mirrors a major fault line in ethics between what are known as consequentialist and deontological theories. For the consequentialist, the morally right action is that which results in the best state of affairs, and the morally wrong action that which results in the worst. The most well-known consequentialist theory is utilitarianism, which we briefly looked at in the previous chapter. Utilitarianism is based on the general happiness principle, which in Jeremy Bentham's formulation is that 'The greatest happiness of the greatest number is the foundation of morals and legislation'. In ethics and in politics, one should do whatever makes the most people happy. This 'whatever' is important, since it signifies that what is important for the utilitarian is the end—increased happiness—not the means, which should be whatever achieves the desired end.

Deontological theories stand opposed to consequentialist ones. For the deontologist, the means is at least as important as the end. So, for example, a deontologist such as Immanuel Kant might say that lying is always morally wrong, even when it results in a greater good. One cannot say the lie was good because it had a good outcome, such as saving an innocent person from being discovered by an assassin, since lying is always wrong and cannot be made right by events having a happy outcome.

In the rhetoric of new Labour, ends have been emphasized. New Labour, we are told, supports 'what works' regardless of ideology. So, for example, if involving the private sector in the delivery of public services leads to better services, then the private sector should be involved. This 'pragmatism' has been criticized for lacking values. But, as should now be clear, stressing ends over means need not be indicative of a lack of values. Rather, it may just show what, for new Labour, is most highly valued—in this case, the end result.

In practice, making any political (or moral) decision, usually involves considering both ends and means, and different people judge differently how important these two factors are. Even new Labour would not use just any means to achieve its goals. It would not, for example, use slave labour to run the health service because that would deliver more efficient public services. For the political observer, the task is to judge whether the balance of ends and means is right. How we judge new Labour's record on this score if not for me to say. But it should be evident that the mere fact that new Labour has laid the stress on the ends does not mean that it has necessarily abandoned all its principles. It is only by reference to principles, after all, that we can judge whether 'what works' really does work and delivers the better society we all want.

Freedom

So far, we have looked at some general features of our emotional responses to new Labour and the relationship between principles and practice. But, of course, political thinking requires consideration of particular values and principles. Two of the most prominent values espoused in political discourse are those of freedom and equality, which, unlike mother and apple pie (both of which have many detractors) almost everyone would agree are good things. Considering freedom first, it is evident that different political factions appeal to the value of freedom to justify very different policies. For example, in global politics, opponents of increased 'free trade' often claim that open markets serve to limit the freedoms of people in developing countries, who are forced to bow to the pressure of multinational corporations.

New Labour has been criticized for being authoritarian and anti-freedom. Perhaps most notably, in its second term, it hurried a post-11 September anti-terror bill through Parliament. In its original form it was to have banned incitement to religious hatred, which some feared would suppress legitimate criticism of religion. Another proposal which had to be watered down was a duty on communications providers to retain data transmitted by clients that the police could access to help their enquiries. What was approved were increased powers giving security services the authority to detain suspected foreign terrorists without charge or trial, which civil liberties campaigner groups criticized for being draconian.

This bill, many argued, only continued the authoritarian trend set in new Labour's first term. For instance, people seeking political asylum from abroad had their freedom of movement controlled and were given vouchers, rather than money, to buy food with, creating stigma and restricting their choice. There have also been attempts—as yet unsuccessful—to further restrict the option of defendants in the law courts to choose trial by jury. As ever, assessing these criticisms fairly requires a good grasp of the facts. But it also requires clarity about the concept at the heart of the debate—freedom.

Any serious discussion of freedom has to include Isaiah Berlin's distinction between positive and negative freedom. Negative freedom is freedom from interference, oppression and restraint. It is called negative freedom because it is about an absence of limits. With negative freedom, we can go about our business as we choose, unhindered by others. Positive freedom, on the other hand, is freedom to do certain things, such as fulfil our potential or work. It may appear at first glance that the difference between the two forms of freedom is trivial: if there are no restraints on you, and so you are free in the negative sense, aren't you free to fulfil your potential, in the positive sense? Not necessarily. Imagine a society totally free in the negative sense. In this society, is a child born to a poor family free to fulfil her potential? Given that the state does not 'interfere' to provide schools, housing, and health, this child is dependent on charity and the efforts of her family. To say this person is free to fulfil her potential has a hollow ring to it. No one is constraining her, but her life choices are very limited. As a society, we may interfere to limit negative freedom, by interfering with tax and legislation, in order to provide such children with more choices and opportunity, thus increasing their positive freedom. In a sense, this is what living in a modern developed society is all about: accepting limits on our negative freedom to increase positive freedom.

There are several major considerations that arise out of accepting this distinction. The first is that we often talk about these two different types of freedom in the same breath as if they were of one and same kind. We talk about freedom from hunger and freedom from oppression, but the two are different beasts. To make the world free from hunger requires active intervention—it is a positive freedom; to make it free from oppression requires simply not oppressing—a negative freedom. We may consider both to be fundamental freedoms, but they are freedoms in radically different senses.

Secondly, there is often a trade-off, both between the two freedoms and between two different forms of the same kind of freedom. This kind of justification is offered for many new Labour reforms. In order, for example, to increase the average citizen's negative freedom to go about her business free from the threat of terrorism, it is necessary to limit the negative freedom of those suspected of terrorism, even if some turn out to be innocent. In order to provide a fair system which allows the positive freedom of 'genuine' asylum seekers to be increased through the opportunity to settle in the UK, the negative freedom of all asylum seekers has to be limited. The accusation, of course, is that these measures limit one kind of freedom to an unacceptable degree. Most totalitarian regimes have used the idea that they are giving the people the freedom to live their lives to the full as a spurious justification for the fact that they are actually limiting their negative freedom too much.

A third point is that there is a need to decide how much value we place on each freedom, and how much we are prepared to sacrifice one in order to increase the other. Just to say we believe in freedom is to hide from this fundamental political, and essentially moral, decision. This is significant because when we complain that a proposed new law will restrict our freedom, we often forget just how much we already accept limitations on freedom and how most of us would say it is good that we do so. One fundamental limit on freedom that we expect everyone to accept is the rule of law, as a safeguard to anarchy and to ensure that everyone is treated equally. So I am not free to keep every penny I earn—I have to pay taxes as the law demands. I accept this limit on my freedom (albeit reluctantly) because I think that as a society we need certain services and provision that can only be funded by taxes. I also accept a limit to my freedom to drive as fast as I like, in the interests of public safety. But what can justify these limits on our freedom?

Limits on freedom

Thinking only of negative freedom, if we were to make a list of all the ways in which such freedom is limited, it would make very long reading indeed. More interestingly, after we had got rid of the freedoms which no sane person would accept—such as freedom to kill, maim, or injure—we would find that many of these restrictions are odd and perhaps inconsistent. For example, I am free to go rock-climbing without safety equipment but not free to drive without a seat belt. I am free to drink myself to an early grave, causing misery and pain to my loved ones, but I am not free to smoke the occasional cannabis joint. I am free to insult the prophet Mohammed but I am not free to insult Christ.

The problem with the law is that it builds up gradually over time according to the whims and concerns of the day and so there is bound to be little consistency about what is subject to legislation and what isn't. To a certain extent, this is inevitable, and it would be idealistic to expect the law to be as rational as a theoretical philosophical system. Nevertheless, in order seriously to think about how to make changes that are for the better, greater theoretical clarity about freedom is essential. Consider how in politics policies are often opposed or supported on the basis that they promote or diminish freedom. In the United States, the large tax cuts of George Bush's first year in the White House—the overwhelming benefits of which went to the top 3 per cent earners—were undertaken against the background of a political ideology which sees taxation as an infringement on freedom which should always be minimized. In Britain, a long-running series of disputes over European Union labour regulations are played out against a background where some see extensive labour rights as an infringement on the freedom to trade and others see them as essential to the freedom of workers.

Common to both debates is an ideological battle over the state's right to limit negative freedom. To make progress in this debate we need to consider carefully under which circumstances it is justifiable so to curtail freedom. Here, the three major justifications are the same as those given to justify a public interest in the private affairs of individuals which were discussed in Chapter 2. This is not surprising since privacy is a form of negative freedom—the freedom to live your life without public scrutiny. The justifications need revisiting here because we are now considering general restrictions on freedom rather than just those concerning the specific issue of privacy.

The first of these is the so-called 'harm principle' proposed by John Stuart Mill, who thought that the only justification for the state restricting the freedom of individuals was to protect others. This is why we are not free to kill or injure, and also why we are not free to say what we like all the time, if what we say harms others. The second justification is that we accept a limit on freedom, not to avoid harm to others, but to benefit society as a whole. So paying tax isn't only a way of avoiding harm to others, but of making society a better place. A third justification is to avoid harm to ourselves, which is presumably why smoking, driving without a seat belt, and eating beef on the bone all are, or have been, subject to legal restriction. As in the privacy example, none of these justifications can be accepted without qualification.

The first, that we are not free to harm others, may seem the least controversial. However, we can harm others in many ways, not all of which are, or even should be, illegal. In a capitalist society, businesses are always trying to cause harm to their competitors. Of course that is not usually the primary intent— making money is—but pursuing this goal does often lead to harming competitors. But lack of intent is not an automatic moral get-out clause. Killing innocent pedestrians may not be my intent if I drive around a busy town centre as fast as I can, but that doesn't excuse my behaviour. I may also cause harm by writing a critical review, or acting in a hurtful way. In this respect, the law is an imprecise and inconsistent means of ensuring that, in the exercise of our freedom, we do not harm others. The law cannot prevent all harm being caused to others. At least partly that is because it is not the law's job to legislate against all that is wrong. Law and morality overlap, but they are not the same thing, as we saw in Chapter 2.

As it happens, where new Labour has sought to limit freedom, it has not on the whole been in order to prevent harm to others. Asylum seekers are not dangerous, and nor will restricting trial by jury increase our security—its goal is merely to make the judicial system more efficient. Only in the case of the anti-terror bill is the primary justification the need to prevent harm. In most other cases, the second justification mentioned above seems to be more important: the restrictions on our freedom are for the greater social good. In order that access to justice is fair and fast and that asylum seekers are treated fairly but not indulgently, we need to create rules that prevent people from doing exactly what they please.

The problem with this kind of justification is that the West has frequently criticized authoritarian regimes around the world and in our own past for using this as a justification for unacceptable oppression. It's not just that we suspect that the limits on freedom are not for the greater social good, but that we feel, even if they were, that would not justify them. So what if the country benefits if people are forced out of their homes to work the fields—no one has the right to force anyone to move anywhere. However, while criticizing others, the same justification is used for albeit much less extreme measures at home.

The point is not that it is never permissible to limit freedom for the greater public good, nor that there is no moral difference between restricting the movements of asylum seekers and forcing people out of their homes. Rather, the point is simply that 'because it is for the greater social good' is not a good reason by itself to limit freedom. The greater social good has to be something significant and real and the infringement on our liberty a reasonable price to pay for it. Here there is room for reasonable people to disagree and for us to reach very different conclusions about the wisdom of various new Labour reforms.

What then of the third justification for limiting freedom—protecting ourselves? It is perhaps surprising that as a society we seem to accept some limits on self-harming behaviour more readily than we do limits on freedom in the name of the greater public good. Seat belts, drug prohibitions, high taxation on cigarettes and alcohol are all largely seen as acceptable, even though they seem only to affect the individuals involved. Some would argue that society as a whole suffers if more people die or sustain serious injury through not wearing seat belts, or contract illness because of smoking. However, these arguments are dubious. For example, the counter-argument that smokers save the state money by both dying young (and thus not using up expensive free health care and pensions) and contributing huge amounts in taxation to the exchequer cannot be dismissed as easily as some like to believe.

Despite the accusation that new Labour is paternalistic, it is for the overall social good rather than our individual personal well-being that most of its reforms have aimed to serve. Indeed, in a surprise move in October 2001, the home secretary, David Blunkett, announced the downgrading of cannabis from a class B to a class C drug, a decidedly non-paternalistic move. New Labour may restrict freedom for the greater social good, but it does not habitually regulate behaviour of individuals for their own good.

The upshot of considering all these ways in which negative freedom is and should be limited is twofold. First, hardly anyone believes in unfettered negative freedom—we all think it has its limits. Secondly, when we examine what justifies these limits, we find at least three very different reasons, which carry different weight in different instances. These two facts together show how the debate around freedom is more complicated than pious slogans suggest and how we should be more cautious about our proclamations about freedom, both when we accuse new Labour of reducing it and claim ourselves to be championing it.

Equality

New Labour has also been criticized for abandoning its traditional commitment to greater equality. To a certain extent new Labour is a victim of its own spin-doctoring here. Before the overtly tax-raising 2002 budget, the party was so keen to reassure middle Britain that it would not over-tax them that it failed to highlight just how redistributive its policies had actually been. Initiatives like the working families tax credit—another idea borrowed from the new Democrats—were crucial here. Independent studies have shown the incomes of the poorest 10 per cent rising at a faster rate than those of the richest, who according to at least one study, carried out by the Institute for Fiscal Studies, actually saw their post-tax incomes fall.

I mention this because it again highlights how important getting the facts right is in these debates, not because these few facts quoted clinch the case. But, as we have repeatedly found, facts have to be understood and here philosophical work can help. In this instance, what is important is to distinguish between different forms of equality.

Socialists have traditionally been concerned with equality of outcome. This means everyone being equally well-off, educated, trained, housed, and so on. This does not mean that everyone should literally have exactly the same as everyone else—what use is a piano to a guitarist, for example? The point is rather that, on balance, everyone's lot should be more or less equal in value to everyone else's. If we want to consider the claim that new Labour has abandoned its commitment to this form of equality, two points already made are important here. First, as Rawls's difference principle makes plain, it is possible to share the aims of those who seek greater equality of outcome, yet accept that there are times when it is better to allow a little more inequality in order to help the worst off. The worst off aren't helped if equality is achieved at the cost of them getting poorer. Second, policies which may seem to be anti-egalitarian in this sense, such as the freeze on higher rates of income tax, may, as part of a package of measures, actually help result in greater equality of outcome. So in order to know if the principle we support is being put into practice, we need to look at the actual results of policy, not just how they appear.

A second form of equality is that of opportunity. This is where everyone is given the same chance to achieve in every aspect of life, be it education, work, sport, or politics. Beyond that, it is up to individual talent and effort how far they achieve their goals. In its pure form, this would result in a 'meritocracy', where those who do best are those with the talent or determination or both to succeed. New Labour has been a champion of meritocracy. The problem here is that equality of outcome and opportunity usually turn out to be in opposition. The whole point about equality of opportunity is precisely that it is up to individuals how well they get on, which inevitably means that there will be unequal outcomes. Like the parable of the talents, give three different people the same opportunity and some will make more from it than others.

The equality issue is easiest for people who are totally committed to either equality of opportunity or equality of outcome. If you think equality of outcome is all that matters, you only need worry yourself about how to achieve it. (In the absence of a willing anarchist community, strong government is the usual choice.) If you think equality of opportunity is all that matters, again, your only concern is how to provide it. If you don't believe in equality of either sort, laissez-fair capitalism—the withdrawal of the state to leave everyone to battle it out economically—is a possible choice.

But most of us value both forms of equality to a certain extent. There is no contradiction involved in thinking there is value in both forms of equality while accepting that having both completely is impossible. What that does mean is that you need to make some difficult choices about how much of each type of inequality is acceptable. For example, you may decide that, although you can accept a political programme that creates inequality of outcome, you would not like your country to have very high levels of such inequality. Rather than trying to square the circle of creating a society where both outcomes and opportunities are distributed equally, one can focus on eliminating unacceptably high levels of both types of inequality. So the question for new Labour is not whether it has furthered equality of opportunity or equality of outcome, but whether its policies achieve the right balance of both.

There are other forms of equality which are also important. Equality of treatment or equality before the law is one. This is about ensuring that everyone has a right to be treated the same, by the law and by society. There is also equality of value, which is the belief that everybody's life is of equal value, that we should not judge the life of one person to be more valuable than that of another. These really are attainable equalities. There is no reason why a society should unfairly give preference to certain individuals or groups over others or value certain individuals or groups over others. If we strove hard to achieve these equalities, we might find that we have created a society in which the need for greater equality of outcome or opportunity was less urgent.

The relationship between these different forms of equality is rather complex. The difficulties are compounded when people also start confusing these concepts of equality with the idea that people have the same level or types of ability, which the evidence strongly suggests they do not. Confusing this with credible forms of equality has caused terrible confusion and even harm. People are reluctant to admit, for example, that some people are more intelligent than others, or that women and men tend to perform better at different tasks (typically women are better are verbal tasks, men at spatial ones). The only reason for this, as far as I can tell, is that people fear that agreeing to these differences will mean endorsing the view that people are of different value or that they should not be given the same level of opportunity or outcome. However these are totally separate issues. It simply doesn't follow that, if they tend to be different, men and women are of unequal value, or that they should not be given the same opportunities. As I have set it out above, credible political notions of equality have nothing to do with people being the same in terms of their abilities, skills, or potential. It is simply a confusion to lump them all together.

As with freedom, then, the concept of equality turns out to be multifaceted, and it seems you cannot have all forms of equality at the same time. So if we are to take seriously the claim that new Labour has abandoned its commitment to equality, we have to look at its record on each type of equality and we also have to expect to find compromises and trade-offs designed to produce the optimal overall package of equality. We also need to look at what its policies have actually resulted in and not rush to conclude that a policy is anti-egalitarian because, on the face of it, it doesn't seem to promote equality.

Conclusion

I want to finish off with a few words about how equality and freedom relate. One could systematically go through the different types of equality and freedom and see which can or can't go together. What we'd find, more often than not, is that we can't have everything. For example, complete negative freedom would not provide equality of opportunity, outcome, or treatment. Free of all constraints, some would be born into opportunity while others were born into misery; some would become rich, others poor; and in the absence of law, some would be treated well, others badly. A high degree of positive freedom may provide more equality of outcome, opportunity, and of treatment, but would severely limit negative freedom and would arguably take the 'opportunity' out of freedom of opportunity. As has been the recurring theme of this chapter, often what you gain in one area you lose in another.

Why is it important to be aware of all these different forms of equality and freedom and how they relate to each other? One reason is that terms like freedom and equality are used to try to gain our support—and to turn us against others. We have seen how new Labour has been accused of turning its back on equality and limiting freedom. But are the accusers themselves neglecting other forms of both freedom and equality in ways which we would not approve of? If we are to avoid being manipulated and if we are to see politicians in their true light and make sound judgements about their policies, then we must wise up to some of the basic distinctions in the language we use to talk about politics. To do this we need to see beyond our emotional attachments and political habits. Philosophy can help us to do this and hopefully contribute to making us wiser political animals.

4

Bush declares all-out war on the havens of terrorism

By Tony Harnden
Washington La Guardia
Editor

allied behind
as Presi-
facing

Hawkes & Doves: The morality of war

The World Trade Centre

On 11 September 2001 I had a hospital appointment in London. As usual, I was kept waiting and ended up being at the hospital for several hours. While I was there, I overheard snippets of conversation, fragments from televisions and radios. I came to be aware that something of significance had happened, without knowing exactly what it was. When the time came to leave I briefly phoned my partner to let her know I was on my way home. I was told the startling news that planes had gone missing and skyscrapers had been attacked in the United States. There was a general sense of confusion, with no one knowing what more was to come and whether similar events would happen elsewhere. I hurried to the underground station and picked up the evening newspaper. There was little yet in it, but what was there was staggering. Two aeroplanes had flown into the twin towers of New York's World Trade Centre and others were missing.

I wanted to get home as soon as possible, not only to distance myself from London's own skyscrapers, but to find out what exactly was going on. I feel uneasy at such times. Was there any morbid voyeurism in my desire to see television reports of the disaster? Mixed with the shock and the horror, was there a little bit of excitement? Many soldiers are said to get a kind of thrill from actual combat. On the underground going home that day I was amazed to see what appeared to be some American tourists having their photo taken with the front page of the evening newspaper, smiling. I am sure that photograph has since been destroyed, its memory an embarrassment.

Once home, I saw the television pictures that have since

immortalized the day. The full story finally emerged. Both towers had collapsed, killing thousands. Another plane had been flown into the Pentagon. A fourth had crashed near Pittsburgh. The worst pictures for me were those of the people trapped in the north tower, having just seen the south tower collapse, calling to the people below. For twenty minutes, they lived with the terror that at any moment they could suffer the same fate. We know now that many spoke to their loved ones on the telephone, and these conversations are perhaps the most poignant reminders of the awfulness of that day. For many others, they could only wait, unable to speak to their partners, their children, their family, and fearing that they would never see or hear from them again. Then, the north tower too collapsed.

The television images were transfixing. But one could only watch the repeated images so many times. The news was followed with unusual avidity for many days to come. Very soon, the same day in fact, the big question became, how was America to react?

The answer is what has come to be known as the war against terrorism. From the start, it was clear that this was not going to be an ordinary war of state against state, but of states against disparate terrorists groups. Bin Laden's al-Qaeda was the first target, but it was never claimed that it would be the only one. 'This is a conflict without battlefields or beachheads, a conflict with opponents who believe they are invisible,' said President George Bush four days after the terrorist attacks. 'Victory against terrorism will not take place in a single battle, but in a series of decisive actions against terrorist organizations and those who harbour and support them.'

While it is true that this war is different, in an important sense all wars are different. The prolonged trench warfare of the First World War was without precedent, and certainly unique in scale. The wars that my country, The United Kingdom, has been involved in over recent years have all been very different. In one, a naval task force sailed halfway around the world to the South Atlantic to reverse an Argentinian invasion of a small colonial island, with significant casualties on both sides. It has contributed to the Allied forces in the Gulf War, a conflict in which air power and 'smart bombs' meant that there were few British casualties but many amongst Iraqi soldiers, both professional and conscript, as well as civilians. The particular combination of terrain and technology that made such a war possible may never occur again. Britain also joined the USA in later bombings of Iraq, which again saw civilian as well as military casualties. More recently, NATO engaged in military conflict in Kosovo in a peacekeeping role which again had no real precedent. So we should not be fooled by the singularity of the war against terrorism into thinking that it shares nothing in common with other wars and conflicts.

As citizens, digesting the news reports and speeches of our political leaders, we make decisions about where we stand on the rights and wrongs of war. If we are opposed, and our opposition is strong, we may campaign against the war. Such campaigning can have an effect, as was shown in America during the Vietnam War. Domestic public opinion is important and for that reason politicians try to shape it and the public has in some sense a responsibility to provide support where support is called for, opposition when opposition is called for.

But how do we decide whether to support our country—or indeed any country—when it enters into an armed conflict? This is a difficult question and any fair decision requires us to know some facts, or at least get as clear a grasp on them as we can. In the war against terrorism, for example, we need to know what the risk of future attacks is; what the effects of military action on regional stability will be; whether the people identified as the culprits really are guilty; what the likely consequences of the action are; its chances of success; the probability and extent of civilian casualties, and so on. The problem is that, in many instances, even experts can determine no more than probabilities, and in times of war, accurate information is often hard to find.

The best we can do is examine the reasons given for entering into the conflict and try to judge, on the basis of the information we have, whether these reasons are sufficient. In the war against terrorism, several reasons have been presented by George Bush and the British prime minister, Tony Blair, to justify the military side of the campaign, operation Enduring Peace, which began with attacks on Afghanistan on 7 October 2001. Here, I want to examine whether these kinds of reasons are sufficient to justify military action and then look at the consequences of these deliberations for the war against terrorism. I am going to focus on what the two main political leaders—Bush and Blair—have actually said to justify the campaign before turning to the principles of just war theory to see how they apply to this conflict.

Punishment

On the day of the terrorist attacks, George Bush said, 'Make no mistake: The United States will hunt down and punish those responsible for these cowardly acts.' Bush was arguing that the American response would be motivated by a form of legal justice: the wrongdoers needed to be found and punished for their crimes. Bush returned to this theme on many occasions, saying, for example, on 19 September, 'It is so important for my fellow Americans, as well as everybody in the world to understand that America will hold those evil-doers accountable.'

There are many reasons why this is an extremely problematic justification for a war. First, as many have pointed out, bringing someone to justice in a legal sense requires capture and fair trial, yet in this instance Bush has repeatedly said that he wants Osama bin Laden 'dead or alive'. Second, the issue of what forms of punishment are justified and on what grounds is a philosophically thorny one.

But even if we accept that punishment is both deserved and can be meted out without trial, that still leaves problems. Consider the 1998 strikes against Iraq as an example. Saddam Hussain, the leader of Iraq, had repeatedly refused to cooperate with United Nations arms inspectors, who had the authority to inspect Iraqi sites for chemical and nuclear weapons. There was a lot of brinkmanship and squaring up to each before Britain and the United States decided they had had enough and sent the bombs in. There are, it seems to me, several plausible justifications for these attacks. But the idea that 'Saddam needed to be punished' is not one of them. It makes the obvious error of confusing a country with its leader. How did bombing Iraq punish

Saddam? He was not bombed. His popularity in Iraq tends to increase when he is attacked by 'the West'. Furthermore, the people who are actually on the receiving end of the bombs are usually not those responsible for the decisions the bombings are designed to be punishment for. You do not punish the chief executive of a corrupt retail business by thumping a sales assistant. You do punish her if you burn down one of her stores, but this is a very crude way of doing so, as the most damage is inflicted on the staff of the now-defunct store and, worse still, anybody unlucky enough to be caught up in the blaze.

In the same way, the desire to punish Osama bin Laden and other members of the al-Qaeda network, however fair, cannot in itself be a justification for a wider armed conflict. This is an important point because wars are often personalized by governments and leaders. If everyone agrees that such-and-such is a nasty, brutal leader and the war is presented as an attack on him, many will agree it is a good thing. But an attack on a country is only an attack on its leader indirectly. The leader may be harmed by it, but often he is not. And even if he is harmed, many others are harmed along the way. We should not be insensitive to this. In films, in the process of the hero fulfilling his or her mission and surviving, many innocent bystanders become machine-gun fodder. We ignore this because it's only a film. We should not be so willing to ignore the deaths of the 'extras' in real-life conflict because we are focusing only on the stars—in this case, the leaders.

In Afghanistan, it might be protested that the attacks have been directed only against the al-Qaeda network, not the whole country. Bush has repeatedly stressed that the war is not against the Afghan people. Tony Blair, speaking to the House of Commons on 8 October 2001, said, as he has done before and since, 'Our argument is not with the Afghan people.' However, the war has involved and harmed more people than just the terrorists. There is an important moral difference between deliberately killing the innocent and accidentally doing so. But when such accidental deaths are foreseeable, moral responsibility cannot be entirely avoided. Following a path which makes this inevitable has to be justified by more than the desire to bring a wrongdoer to justice. Of course, it does not follow from this that it is always wrong to engage in conflicts where civilians and conscripts die. It is merely to say that to defend an armed conflict on the grounds that it punishes an individual leader is not of itself an inadequate justification when others are also harmed.

National self-interest

We often hear leaders appeal to the national self-interest. This has not been such a prominent feature of the war against terrorism, but, nonetheless, Tony Blair did say at the start of operation Enduring Peace, 'We can see since the 11th of September how economic confidence has suffered, with all that means for British jobs and British industry. Our prosperity and standard of living, therefore, require us to deal with this terrorist threat.'

There is one obvious respect in which national self-interest is a vital factor—namely, when the citizens of a country are threatened by hostile aggressors. In the same speech, Blair had talked about self-defence. But the national self-interest includes factors other than this and is surely not a sufficient justification of war.

Consider the first Gulf War. What if it were true that the only justification for the war was that it would keep oil prices down, which was in the interests of the allied nations? If this were the truth, then surely that would have made the war morally bankrupt. What is worse, it would mean that the allied forces had no greater motive for repelling that Iraqi invasion than the Iraqis had for undertaking it, as it was done, after all, in the Iraqis' self-interest. A world in which nations were justified for going to war whenever it was to their advantage to do so would be a barbaric and uncivilized one. Both parties in a war would be equally justified for taking part, so long as they could claim it was in their own interests to do so. You could say goodbye to good guys and bad guys, because war would effectively be every country for itself.

The inadequacy of this justification is made most apparent by analogy to individuals. It is obviously not justifiable for me to kill another person because it is in my self-interest to do so. Self-interest just isn't a sufficient justification for killing. So why has national self-interest sometimes been flagged up as a reason to go to war? In the war against terrorism, national self-interest has not been appealed to very much. Perhaps the only reason why it was mentioned at all—and one reason why it is often included among justifications for war—is that governments want their citizens to feel that the war has something in it for them. Noble moral goals may not stir people to support a war; the fear that their quality of life might suffer could sometimes be a more effective spur to solidarity.

Perhaps, then, the justification is purely rhetorical. However, it should be said, against this, that many believe that nations usually, if not always, go to war only for the national self-interest, but are at pains to deny this and dress up their motivations in more morally uplifting ways. This cynical view deserves serious consideration. Although it is hard to assess the truth of the claim directly, what we can do is ask what would be the case if it were true. Given that I have argued that the national self-interest is not in itself enough to justify war (except in the case of self-defence) it might seem that adopting this view should make us oppose any wars which are thus motivated. However, it is not as simple as that.

Means, motives, and consequences

Let us suppose it is true that nations tend to go to war when it is in their self-interest to do so. That in itself does not mean that no wars are ever justified, for two reasons. First, no matter how cynical we become about motives for war, experience should only teach us caution in accepting what our leaders say about the goals and motivations for going to war. It does not mean that, by necessity, all wars must be only about self-interest. When someone has lied repeatedly, it means we should treat what they say in the future with caution, not that everything they say will be untrue.

The second reason is perhaps more powerful, namely, that sometimes the best interests of others and our own self-interest coincide. Take for example a frequently rehashed movie scenario, where someone can only inherit a huge personal fortune if they manage to spend one million dollars in twenty-four hours. If this person spends the money on a good cause, should we oppose this because doing so is in his own self-interest? I don't think we should. In fact, it would be perverse to try to dissuade people from doing good deeds whenever it is in their self-interest to do so. Of course, in such cases it may well affect how much we praise these people or give them credit for their work. The person who gives in order to inherit more is not a person who deserves great credit (except in so far as he could have spent the money on something useless), but that doesn't mean we should not encourage him to do so.

How does this relate to war? Well, we may be cynical about the motives of our political leaders, but if by acting out of self-interest they increase the common good, then we should encourage them, not oppose them. If (and there are a lot of ifs in this scenario) it is the case that the allies liberated Kuwait for purely selfish motives, but that liberating Kuwait was a morally desirable thing to do, then despite deploring their motives, we can back the military action. Similarly, if the attacks in Afghanistan had been motivated by pure self-interest, but would still have achieved good, the action should not have been opposed.

This argument depends upon a distinction which not everyone would agree is reasonable. I have distinguished between the morally desirable outcome and the intention of the agent—in this case a nation—who acts to bring about that outcome. For the sake of simplicity, let's refer to these as outcome and intention respectively. I have suggested that one can approve of the outcome while disapproving of the intention, and that, furthermore, one can be justified in encouraging someone to do something that brings about a desirable outcome even though their motives for doing so are morally repugnant. (Note that this is not the same as claiming that *any* means is justified to achieve a desirable end. I shall return to this later.) As we saw in Chapter 2, some would object to this on the grounds that motivation is at least as important in ethics as outcomes.

To see why this might be so, imagine a world in which everything is controlled so that whenever someone tries to harm someone else, the effect is just the opposite, and that when they try to help others, they end up harming them. If everyone in this world is self-serving and out to get others, the result will be a world where everything turns out for the best. But is this a world of which we would approve? Would we say that it is a morally good world? Our intuitions would suggest it is not, because all the people in it are cruel and self-serving. This is evidence that morality is not just about outcomes but also about character. And so it is important to condemn actions that are immorally motivated, even if they result in good things.

To further strengthen this case, consider the case of the person who attempts to murder an innocent person. By mistake, he shoots the wrong person. But this wrong person turns out to have been on the verge of detonating a doomsday weapon that would wipe out humanity. So the outcome was good. But surely that doesn't mean it would have been right to encourage this man to try to murder an innocent?

These arguments are interesting, but to my mind inconclusive. In the second example, if you could know for sure what the outcome would be, and this was the only way the would-be agent of genocide could be killed, I would say it would be right to encourage him to carry out the killing. Our reluctance to approve of this stems, I believe, from the fact that in real life we cannot know for sure what would happen and the fact that we would have actively to encourage someone to behave with murderous intent. However, the case of war is disanalogous in two ways. First, though war is unpredictable, we are not relying on mistakes to achieve what we think is desirable. Secondly, in the case of war, we can both support the war and make clear our motivation for doing so. We need not encourage our leaders to act out immoral desires—we can encourage them to act for better motives. We may fail, but we have both furthered the end we approve of and argued against motivations we feel lack moral justification.

The first example seems trickier, but I think it too is inconclusive. The argument about this strange world where wickedness results in goodness merely shows that we don't want a world full of wicked people, even if that world turns out to be a wonderful place to live. That may be enough to show intentions are indispensable in ethics, but it provides no reason to suppose that supporting good outcomes but condemning bad intentions will, on average, make for a world with people more generally motivated by immoral desires. Intentions are important, and that is why, if we support a war, we should make it clear that our motivations are not those of pure self-interest. We should encourage good intent as well as good consequences. I can't see why we can't do that if we praise the outcome but criticize the intent.

One final consideration here is that some may argue that when we are dealing with the political sphere, where many, many people are affected, we should be more instrumental than we are in private morality. It may be a good thing to make a stand on a matter of principle, even though a few people are worse off as a result. But if a political action affects thousands or millions, it is arguable that the interests of those people override any requirement to retain 'moral integrity'. To see why, consider this example.

A wealthy businessman wishes to be honoured by the state. He makes an offer to the prime minister, who can decide such things, to make a large donation to charity in return for the honour. Most of us would feel the prime minister should reject the deal. But what if he offers to provide clean water for a small Third World country? In this case, we may feel that the prime minister's refusal to go along with this scheme would be irresponsible. Despite the fact that this is a kind of bribe, many would feel the prime minister would be sacrificing the livelihoods of thousands of people just in the name of an ethereal thing we call 'principle' or 'integrity'. In this case, the good outcome of acting in an underhand way seems so good that it justifies going along with it. After all, surely relieving poverty is more important than a state honour, or the clean conscience of one individual? Similarly, we might not want our political leaders to uphold certain moral principles in times of conflict if people are harmed as a result. We must not fall prey to what Bernard Williams calls 'moral self-indulgence'.

These considerations together suggest that a justified cynicism about the motives and characters of political leaders should not in and of itself lead us to stand against all war. We can disbelieve the sincerity of the speeches of George Bush and Tony Blair. But what we need to determine is whether the war is just, not whether these are two good men.

Anti-appeasement

On 20 September 2001, George Bush declared that 'The civilized world is rallying to America's side. They understand that if this terror goes unpunished, their own cities, their own citizens may be next.' Bush was raising the spectre of appeasement, the fear that, if we do not stand up to wrongdoing now, further and greater wrongdoing will only follow later. Horrible though war is, it is sometimes necessary to kill in order to prevent even worse bloodshed in the future.

There are two historical examples commonly used to demonstrate this: one actual and one counterfactual. The first is Hiroshima. Defenders of the dropping of the A-Bomb on the town of Hiroshima in Japan claim that it hastened the end of the Second World War in the Pacific. While it was horrendous that thousands of people died in the blast and for years after because of its side effects, the truth is that even more would have died if the war had dragged on. The Japanese would not have surrendered—it would have been too great a dishonour—unless they were shown the truly horrendous consequences of not doing so. (There is, of course, a line of argument which disputes that Hiroshima actually saved lives. For the sake of this argument, the reader needs to set this aside and ask, *if* Hiroshima did save lives in the long run, would that make it morally justified?)

Those who find this doesn't justify the horror of Hiroshima should ask themselves why it is that Hiroshima is more horrific than even more people dying in a protracted war. The worry is that the thought of the huge, concentrated devastation of the A-bomb simply lands more of an emotional punch than the thought of many more individual deaths. Likewise, twenty people dead in a train crash make the news, whereas twenty-five separate road deaths do not. But, of course, a pile of twenty dead bodies represents less of a cost in human terms than twenty-five spread-out deaths.

The second example often used is that of Hitler. If the British and the French had stood up to Hitler earlier on, there would have been a shorter war with a couple of hundred, maybe a few thousand deaths, but not a six-year conflict and the genocide of six million Jews. Though it may have seemed bloodthirsty to start a war over, say, the Sudetenland, it would, in the long run, have saved many millions of lives to have done so.

In the case of the war against terrorism, the argument here is that terrorist groups are increasingly able to kill innocent civilians. What we saw on 11 September was just the first case of a new kind of mass killing. If we do nothing to stem the growth of these terrorist groups, they will strike again, perhaps with even worse consequences. Imagine a nuclear device in London, for example, or germ warfare in Washington. To prevent these disasters we have to crush the terrorist groups before it is too late, even if that does mean a bloody war. Less blood now will result in more blood later.

To those who support these arguments, they often seem irresistible. The only way out seems to be to assert a suicidal pacifism: yes, it may be true that you can kill now and save lives later, but it is always wrong to kill so even if the consequences are terrible, you mustn't kill. Pacifism is an important position and so I shall return to it in more detail a little later. But there are other responses to the anti-appeasement argument. The first, and most obvious, is that though one may support the principle of anti-appeasement, there is still the question of whether in fact any particular conflict will prevent worse harm in the future. Because so many people agree that it is better to stand up early than pay later, the argument is often wheeled out as an argument for war, even though it is highly doubtful whether the principle truly applies. So while we may agree with the logic of anti-appeasement, we might doubt whether the campaign in Afghanistan, for example, really did reduce the terrorist threat or whether it just created more people sympathetic to al-Qaeda's goals.

We also have to be on our guard against propaganda here. A government which seeks public support for its actions will talk up the threat posed by the country it is attacking and then ask us, 'Would you want us to ignore this threat?' On several occasions the FBI issued warnings that it had intelligence pointing to 'imminent' terrorist attacks on the USA or US interests which did not materialize. One must wonder whether these warnings are periodic attempts to maintain support for the military campaigns, genuine intelligence reports, or both.

But let us suppose that, in fact, the sums have been done correctly, and that to the best of anyone's knowledge, it really does look as though the military campaigns against terrorists will save lives in the long run. Could only a complete pacifist defy the logic that points towards war? The answer is no. To see why, we have to consider again the question of how far means justify ends. In general, we don't tend to believe that the end always justifies the means. For example, let us say I wish to buy a new car. If I steal money as a means to achieving that end, most people would consider that wrong. Even if the end is more morally worthy than car-ownership, similar principles apply. Most people would think it was normally wrong to steal money from another person (unless perhaps they were rich), even if that money was used to help people in need.

On the other hand, sometimes we accept that it is justifiable to resort to devious means to achieve worthy ends. Stealing from someone who won't miss the money in order to save a person from starvation is a classic example. So is, for some people, assassinating a deranged leader who will kill many people. While normally such acts of theft and murder are considered wrong, in these cases the end to which they are a means is so worth attaining that they become morally justifiable.

If we agree with this general line of thought, then we are advocating a quite sophisticated moral position, where the rightness or wrongness of an action is partly dependent on its overall consequences (saving lives) and partly dependent on either its immediate consequences (depriving someone of their property or life), the rightness or wrongness of the act in itself (theft, murder), or a combination of both. There are some cases where the end justifies the means and others where it does not. Formulating rules for distinguishing between the two types of cases is certainly a tricky business. For our purposes, we need only consider one case: why might some feel that starting a war is an unacceptable means of preventing greater suffering in the long run, assuming that they are not pacifists and would fight if attacked in the future?

One answer to this question might be that it is very important to respect individual life. As Kant put it, we must always treat people as ends in themselves and never merely as means. So, for example, in the case of Hiroshima it seems morally repugnant that we could 'trade in' the lives of innocent civilians in order to 'buy' the saving of more lives in the future. Doing this arguably treats human lives as units of value, rather like money, which can be traded to achieve the best overall result. Once we start this way of thinking about human life we lose the sense of what really gives human life its value in the first place—the fact that each person is an irreplaceable, autonomous individual.

However, it is not obvious that not dropping the A-Bomb shows any greater respect for individual human lives. Could we not equally say that not dropping the bomb would have been 'trading in' the lives of conscripts and fewer civilians in order to save the lives of the civilians the Hiroshima bomb killed? If America gave up on its war against terrorism, would it be giving up the lives of future victims of terrorist attacks in order to save the lives of those involved with the conflict now?

There is one more vital consideration. In working out whether it is better to suffer casualties now or later, we have to remember that there is an asymmetry in the calculation. Going to war means that future fatalities are almost certain: we know that the war against terrorism has and will have a human cost. Not going to war means that there will probably, or possibly, be more casualties later: we fear but do not know that many lives will be lost in future attacks. In comparing the risks, therefore, we are not directly comparing like with like. There is more certainty that death will result from one course of action than the other.

There are no easy solutions to these problems. What we can say is that there are good reasons to oppose appeasement, but one must first judge that the course of action one opposes really is appeasement. We can also say that judging whether it is right to strike now need not rely on crudely comparing the death tolls each course of action is likely to result in.

This does suggest a justification for the war against terrorism, namely that we have to have decisive military action now, even though many will die, including civilians, because, if we don't, the world will not be a safe place to live in. The threat does seem very real. Unchecked, surely the people behind the 11 September attacks would strike again. With nuclear, chemical, or biological capabilities, the results could be even more horrific. But two questions remain. The first is how many people will die in the war against terrorism to prevent this future becoming a reality, and is this proportionate? The second is, can the war against terrorism, as it is currently being waged, remove this threat anyway? These are both questions that can only be answered with facts and information, not philosophy. But what we do with these facts does to some extent depend upon how we use philosophy to assess the rights and wrongs of anti-appeasement policies.

Just war

So far, we have looked at what the politicians have said about their reasons for going to war and assessed their strength. An alternative strategy is to start with a framework that tells us whether a war is just or not and then apply this to individual conflicts to see if they pass the test. One such framework goes under the name of just war theory. Versions of this have their origin in the writings of Augustine and Islam and although the theory is not accepted by all philosophers, there is a remarkable degree of support for many of its central principles.

Just war theory sets two tests for any conflict. In order for the war to be just, first there must be *jus ad bellum*—in other words, there have to be good reasons to wage the war. Second, there must also be *jus in bello*—in other words, the war must be fought in a morally correct way.

Interestingly, in his key speeches at the start of operation Enduring Peace, the British prime minster, Tony Blair, set out a justification in a way which has striking parallels to just war theory. Consider this extract from his statement to the House of Commons on 8 October 2001:

We took almost four weeks after 11 September to act. I pay tribute to President Bush's statesmanship in having the patience to wait. This was for three reasons. First, we had to establish who was responsible. Once it was clear that the al-Qaeda network planned and perpetrated the attacks we then wanted to give the Taliban regime time to decide their own position: would they shield Bin Laden or yield him up? It was only fair to give them an ultimatum and time to respond. It is now clear they have chosen to side with terrorism. But thirdly, we wanted time to make sure that the targets for any action, minimised the possibility of civilian casualties.

The first two reasons Blair gave correspond to two key aspects of *jus ad bellum*. One is the requirement that the war is fought in a just cause. In emphasizing the need to establish who the culprits were for the terrorist attacks, Blair acknowledged this essential requirement of just war theory. The second is that war be started only as a last resort. In stressing that the USA had given time for the Taliban to respond to its demands, Blair was showing how the USA had pursued other avenues before resorting to war.

Blair's third reason takes him into *jus in bello*. A key requirement for the engagement in a just war is that there must be discrimination between legitimate targets and innocent civilians. Blair's speech tried to reassure us that this need for discrimination was being taken very seriously.

There are other principles of just war theory which we can also measure the war against terrorism up against. In regard to *jus ad bellum*, the war must be fought by a legitimate authority, it must be likely to succeed, and it must do more good than harm. These last two conditions are particularly hard to apply. To decide if they are met requires us to consider the best information we have and not just engage in abstract reasoning.

There is a final component of *jus ad bellum*: that those waging the war are acting on the just cause principle. In other words, a just cause cannot be used as an excuse to pursue some unjust end, such as the occupation of another country. This has been used as an argument against Israel in the Six Day War of 1967. Many agreed that Israel had the right to strike first to defend its territories, but having done so it unjustly remained in occupied land, some of which, including the West Bank, it still holds today. The cause was just, but it was used for unjust ends. This has significance for the earlier discussion on politicians' motives. One reason for not supporting a war which is not justly motivated, even if there is a just motive for the same war, is that the goal being pursued is not the just one, but another, unjust one. We might accept this, but it still seems to me that if the same goal is desired for just and unjust reasons, we may approve of an action which others are undertaking for the unjust reasons, as long as our motivation for doing so is just. Only if our just reason is being used to support an unjust end should we withdraw our approval.

The other main part of *jus in bello*, in addition to the need to discriminate between legitimate and illegitimate targets, is that military action is proportionate. Although mistakes have been made, at the time of going to press it does seem that the war against terrorism had been waged with reasonable restraint. Of course, if one disagrees that the war is just at all, nothing about how it is conducted will be justified. But if one believes the cause is just, with some exceptions (such as the alleged mistreatment of prisoners of war transferred to the US detention centre in Guantanamo Bay, Cuba in January 2002) the manner in which the war had been conducted does not seem to have involved any excess.

The principles of just war theory give us a matrix for assessing whether the war against terrorism is justified or not. If we both use that matrix and at the same time assess the principles behind the justifications our political leaders have made, we have made some progress towards being able to make a better judgement of the war's rights and wrongs.

Pacifism

Finally, however, we must turn to the most extreme opposition to war: pacifism. Pacifism is usually understood as a moral opposition to all violence, although it could in a narrower sense be taken to be opposition to all war, but not all violence. Let us take a mid-range definition of pacifism as the moral opposition to the non-voluntary taking of human life. (The non-voluntary part is intended to leave suicide and euthanasia as separate issues.) For a pacifist, it doesn't matter what the consequences are, it is wrong to kill, period. Even if humanity is wiped out, it is better that we do not kill.

What could motivate such a view? It could be a question of rights: that no one has a right to kill another person. It could be that it is felt that the act of killing is just in and of itself wrong. Or it could be that human life is viewed as sacred and can therefore never be taken. Each of these justifications could be the subject of a lengthy enquiry in its own right, but for now I simply wish to point out some of the issues that must be settled if they are to be seriously examined.

First, when we say no one has a right to kill another person, we must get clear what we mean by rights. One particular difficulty seems to be that rights are often taken to be conditional upon the person respecting the rights of others. If someone abuses the right to liberty, by going around killing people, for example, we feel justified in infringing their right to be free. If someone abuses their right to free speech by inciting unwarranted hatred, we feel entitled to restrict their right of free speech. So the question must be asked, why isn't it the case that one's right to life is forfeited if one does not respect the right of others to live? In other words, isn't war justified if it is waged against a group who kill the innocent? It may turn out that the answer collapses into one of the other two justifications for pacifism: that murder is in and of itself wrong or that life is sacred. In this case, it will turn out that the language of rights is nothing more than a shorthand one of the other two justifications for pacifism.

The first of these is that murder is and of itself wrong. The idea of actions just being wrong is an old one, but hard to pin down. Can we really talk of an action just being wrong, without paying any attention to its consequences? For example, isn't murder wrong precisely because it has the consequence of ending life? But if this is the reason why it is wrong, then if the consequences are different the morality of the action may change. If the consequences of a killing are that, though the life of a killer is ended, an innocent life is saved, surely the morality of that action is different from that of a murder motivated purely by hatred?

Actions can be seen as wrong regardless of consequence on certain religious conceptions of morality. If God just says, 'murder is wrong' then murder is wrong, period. However, it should be noted that, on the one hand, most people do not take religious justifications to be sufficient in assessing the rightness or wrongness of an action, and on the other, that killing is actually totally prohibited by very few religions. In fact, historically, religions have often been among the most fervent supports of wars. If pacifists are not believers of a pacifist religion, then they need to find another reason to back their view that the act of killing is in and of itself wrong, regardless of consequences.

Similar thoughts apply to the idea that life is sacred. On one level, this is a mere platitude. If it means life is of great value, and that individual lives are irreplaceable, few would disagree. But for the pacifist it must mean more: it must mean that life can never be taken since the taking of that life is a terrible wrong which cannot be outweighed by any resulting good. As with the preceding case, finding a justification for this belief outside specific religious beliefs may be quite hard. There are also other problems with this view. First, if we do indeed value life so highly, couldn't that equally be held up as a reason for taking decisive action to save life, even if that means killing some violent aggressors to do so? If life is so precious, surely it should be defended, by force if necessary? The worry is that, again, one justification is really a cover for others: it is not so much that life is sacred but that killing is just wrong or we have no right to kill, which leads us back to problems already discussed.

The second problem is one of consistency. If life is sacred and must never be taken, that rules out euthanasia and suicide too. It means that no matter how much a person is suffering, we may not end their life. That is because, if we do so, we are admitting that there is a difference between a life worth living and a life not worth living, and life is no longer sacred but something which can vary in value. To adopt the sanctity of life view therefore requires commitments in the areas of euthanasia, suicide, and abortion.

Another issue of consistency here is the question of what type of life is sacred: only human life? All animal life? All life, including bacteria and amoebas? The slogan 'life is sacred' is an appealing one, but unless we are to award this sanctity to even single cells—which is surely an absurdity—we must decide what forms of life are sacred and which are not. It may prove to be surprisingly hard to draw a line which stands up to rational scrutiny.

Pacifism, if it is to be credible, must therefore be based on something other than simple ideas about life's sanctity, the moral wrongness of killing, and the right to life.

Conclusion

It can be easy to criticize the words of leaders during wartime. Take, for instance, this proclamation from George Bush, the gist of which he repeated several times: 'Every nation, in every region, now has a decision to make. Either you are with us, or you are with the terrorists.' This is nonsense, of course. You do not either support US action or support the terrorists. It is more than possible to be opposed to al-Qaeda and want it destroyed, but to oppose the US action in Afghanistan, for example.

One could pick up on many phrases like this in the speeches of Tony Blair and George Bush, apply a bit of philosophy to them, and show how they are intellectually paper-thin. This may make us feel clever, but it is not very helpful. For one thing, it makes the mistake of taking something which serves a particular rhetorical function and treating it as though it were a piece of philosophical argument. Leaders need to stir their citizens more than they need to make logically valid deductions.

It is more helpful, I think, to focus on those proclamations that present a prima facie plausible justification for military action, give them the most charitable interpretation, and then see how they stand up. That is what I have attempted to do in this chapter. Some of these justifications have been found to be wanting, such as those that cite the need to punish al-Qaeda or serve the national self-interest. But these arguments have not been the most salient ones in the speeches of Bush and Blair.

Appeals to self-defence, to avoid appeasement, and the need to dispense justice have been stressed more. The first two of these can be legitimate reasons for war. There is also some evidence of a genuine concern to ensure any conflict is fought according to the principles of just war theory.

What is needed to move from these theoretical considerations to a decision on whether to support the war or not are the facts about the threats, risks, intentions, and consequences of the various options available. A philosopher can help to lay bare and examine the principles and justifications invoked to support a war. But whether these principles and justifications actually obtain requires us to look at words and deeds. At that point, the philosopher needs to retire and let others come to their final judgements.

5

Scientists clone human embryos

By Nigel Hawkes
Health Editor
and David Brown
....

SCIENTISTS at an American
have cloned the first

West, founder of the company
and co-author of an article on
the experiments in the Journal
of Regenerative Medicine.

"Scientifically, biologically,
the entities we are creating are
not individuals. They're only
cellular life. They're not
an life," Dr West said. I
er be some tim

Test-tube trouble: Science under fire

Saviour or scourge?

I remember a recent radio discussion where one of the participants expressed the view that modern society had placed science on a pedestal and that we all too uncritically accept what 'science' says as true, which, he thought, was a Bad Thing. Another participant completely disagreed. He felt we lived in a society that was disturbingly anti-science and that the prevailing image people have of scientists is of sinister people in white coats messing around with nature. This, he felt, was a Bad Thing. The disagreement highlights the strange position science finds itself in at the start of the twenty-first century. In some respects we do look up to science. The reason why you often see men and women in white coats in soap powder and cosmetics ads is because the marketing folk have good reasons to believe we see scientists as sources of authority. But, on the other hand, we are also deeply suspicious of scientists and extremely perturbed by the direction some science seems to be taking.

Consider, for example, the deep public mistrust of science which has followed the 'mad cow' crisis in the United Kingdom and Europe. Mad cow disease, or bovine spongiform encephalopathy (BSE), to give it its proper name, is a disease which affects the central nervous system of cows. It is believed that BSE-infected meat in the human food chain is the cause of variant Creutzfeldt–Jakob disease (vCJD), the human form of BSE. Sufferers of vCJD usually first become anxious or depressed. Their behaviour changes, often becoming aggressive. Then, coordination is affected. Patients become clumsy, drop things, or fall over. Finally, cognitive functions such as memory start to be impeded. Sufferers can no longer make sense of the world around them. There is no cure and the disease is fatal. By the end of 2001, over 100 people had died of vCJD in Britain. The leading theory for how the BSE epidemic started is that remains of sheep infected with scrapie—which was not thought to be a hazard to human health—were contained in cattle feed.

This sorry tale has many villains. In the public eye, science is one of them. The official government inquiry into BSE, published on 26 October 2000, criticized the government for spending too long consulting with experts, on whom it relied too much, before implementing advice. If it was a mistake to rely on scientific experts, then that suggested to many that scientists should not be trusted. There was also a widespread perception that the cautious and non-committal reports of scientists indicated a failure in the early identification of a link between BSE and vCJD, or to recognize that there was a serious risk to human health. Any sensible person could see that it could not be healthy to feed sheep remains to herbivores such as cows. Why didn't scientists just come out and say this earlier?

Later events have not increased public confidence. In November 2001, a £217,000 research project to investigate the possibility that BSE had spread from cows to sheep had to be abandoned when it was revealed scientists had probably mixed up sheep and cow brain samples. Two separate inquiries, costing £55,000, could not even determine for certain if such a mix-up had occurred, though it did conclude that there was evidence of bad practice. There was also a scare in January 2002 that infected polio vaccines had caused the vCJD outbreak, which would have located the causes of the disease literally in the scientists' laboratories.

Science has also been put in the dock for its work on human cloning. On 25 November 2001, scientists in Massachusetts announced the first ever cloning of a human embryo. The stated goal of the experiment was not to create cloned infants, but to further research into human therapeutic cloning, which it is hoped may lead to further treatments and cures of serious diseases, such as Alzheimer's and Parkinson's. What was created was no more than a six-cell cluster, but the news still sent a shiver down many spines. The US Senate majority leader, Tom Daschle, described the breakthrough as 'disconcerting', saying he thought it was a move 'in the wrong direction'. The national director of the UK-based Society for the Protection of Unborn Children called it 'a very disturbing and deplorable development'.

Human cloning and the BSE crisis have certainly contributed to growing unease about science and a mistrust for the authority of scientific claims. How far is this mistrust justified? To answer this question we need to look beyond the specifics of BSE and human cloning. In both cases, the specific concerns which arise are symptoms of, and contributions to, wider worries about the general role of science. In the BSE crisis, a major concern is simply that scientists cannot be trusted to get it right. Scientists tell us something is safe, and it is not; or something is unsafe but they are unable or unwilling to confirm this. In the human cloning case, scientists are accused of hubris. They play God and meddle with things that are best left alone. This hubris can also be seen in the BSE case, where the feeding of sheep remains to cattle was deemed safe by scientists, even though it was evidently unnatural. In both cases, the fear is that science has caused more harm than good. Scientific meddling with the 'natural' order is a danger to us all.

So we have at least three objections to assess: that scientific findings are unreliable, that scientists are guilty of playing God, and that science is the cause of serious harms. Philosophy has a role in dealing with all of them.

Harm and responsibility

The question of whether science causes harm might seem to be an empirical rather than a philosophical one. To the extent that the answer to this requires a kind of catalogue of science's effects, this is true. But the very notions of responsibility and harm require philosophical analysis. Consider responsibility first. Many scientists would say that they are rarely, if ever, responsible for harms or benefits to society. Responsibility lies with those who use scientific findings. This is a strong defence in the BSE case. All that scientists did throughout the history of the epidemic was report on what the best evidence concerning the disease was. It was the government and its agencies which decided how to act on this. Indeed, the official report into BSE does not blame scientists at all. It does criticize the government's reliance on experts, but this is a criticism of the government's failure to take action and responsibility, not of those experts' advice.

Even in the human cloning case, scientists can claim to be morally neutral. It is for society and government to set the rules which determine what kind of research can be carried out or not. Scientists should not and do not make these judgements, they just work within the legislative framework provided by others.

This second defence is less persuasive. One cannot evade *moral* responsibility by appeal to purely *legal* principles. For example, if I find a way of legally swindling you out of a lot of money, I cannot claim that my action is morally acceptable just because it is legal. As we saw in greater detail in Chapter 2, questions of legality and morality must be kept separate. So scientists cannot evade their moral responsibility by saying that they only act within the law. If a scientist finds that they are legally able to do something morally wrong, then we can still criticize them if they do it.

The problems of the first defence are more subtle. The defence works by appeal to the moral principle of double effect. This principle states that someone only does wrong, and is thus morally responsible for any harm caused, if they both caused and intended the harm. (This view is associated with deontological moral theories. See Chapter 4 for more on these.) In some instances, this seems fair enough. If I cause a road accident by being so attractive that a driver who sees me walking along the street loses concentration (a very unlikely scenario, I confess), it seems very harsh to say I am responsible for the accident. But the principle of double effect also covers cases when the harm is foreseen. For example, if I put on a show at a busy junction, I may intend only to entertain drivers but I should be able to foresee that my distractions might cause an accident. If I still put the show on and there was an accident, most people would say I was at least partly responsible for it. But according to the principle of double effect, I'm not.

In the BSE case, the defence is that scientists are not responsible for the consequences that follow the publication of their findings. If we accept the principle of double effect, we would have to agree that this defence works. Unless the scientists intended to deceive the public as to the risks of BSE, they are not responsible if, in fact, these risks are not properly dealt with. Since no one seriously charges scientists with deception in this case, the defence thus stands. If we reject the principle of double effect and say that one is responsible only if one can foresee the consequences of one's actions, then the question becomes: should the scientists have seen that the evidence they gave would contribute to an inadequate response to the threat of BSE? There seems no reason to suggest this is true. Furthermore, it is not even true that scientists themselves should know what the proper policy implications of their findings are anyway. Even if they could foresee how their evidence would help shape policy, they would have been in no position to judge whether these policies would have good or bad effects.

We could reject both parts of the principle of double effect—foresight and intention—and say that people are responsible for the consequences of their actions, even if they neither foresee nor intend these consequences. The argument here would be that, although there is nothing harmful in the scientific research as such, because it led to harm, its authors are morally responsible. The main problem here is that, in general, this is too harsh a doctrine. For example, what if I decide to phone someone and, unknown to me, they are driving and my call distracts them, causing them to crash? I did not intend or foresee these consequences and it would seem extremely unfair to hold me responsible for them. If the harm had been foreseeable, that might lead some blame to be laid at my door. But when harms are both unforeseen and unforeseeable, I am surely guiltless.

A second problem is that chains of cause and effect are extremely complex. Many factors led to the mishandling of the BSE crisis. It is true that the scientific reports were part of what Ted Honderich calls the total 'causal circumstance'—roughly, all the factors which together were required in order for the effect to follow. But so are many other factors, such as how government departments were arranged, how tired a certain official may have been on one particular day, whether the post was delivered on time, and so on. We do not normally say that someone is morally responsible just because his actions contributed in some way to the causal circumstance of something bad. The contribution has to be crucial or decisive in some way. In this case, the reactions of the government, rather than the information provided by scientists, seems to be the critical factor.

Scientists cannot then avoid moral responsibility by appealing to the legality of their actions. But nor can they be held to account whenever scientific findings are used inappropriately. Although the details have not been worked out here, unless the harms caused by science are a direct result of what scientists do, perhaps with intent or foresight, it is not scientists who are to blame when things go wrong. Because, as a matter of fact, scientists rarely do directly cause such harms, it is therefore usually wrong to blame scientists when scientific evidence is used badly. The reasons why scientific evidence often *is* used badly will be considered later.

Harm without responsibility

One might accept that *scientists* themselves should not be held responsible for things like the BSE fiasco, but nonetheless identify *science* as a cause of too many of our problems. Science is a kind of loose cannon that must be kept in check in order to prevent its harmful consequences from damaging society.

Whether this is true or not must largely be an empirical question. The extreme view—that we would be better off without science at all—is extremely implausible. Imagine science had been banned in 1800. Would the world today be, on balance, a better or a worse place? There would certainly be more disease and shorter life expectancy. We would also be living in a comparatively un-cosmopolitan world, as travel would still be difficult and time-consuming. If you're a Westerner more impressed with Chinese herbal medicine than orthodox medicine, then remember that the great international interchange of ideas we enjoy now is largely down to ease of communication. And you also have to remember that a lot of our problems are not caused by science, but by nature. Two hundred years ago, in a much less scientifically advanced age than our own, mortality rates were much higher and women routinely died in childbirth. So if we did stop science in 1800, we would have to expect earlier deaths by natural causes than we are used to.

A more credible view is not that, on balance, we would be better off without science, but that science is sufficiently dangerous that, in order to benefit from it, we have to be constantly on our guard against its excesses. These excesses include the hubris of human cloning and the disregard of common sense that suggested feeding sheep remains to cows was healthy.

This sounds reasonable, but the argument fails to single out what is especially dangerous about science. To give an example, the same argument could be used against something beloved of many sceptical of science—alternative medicine. I think it is perfectly reasonable to say that alternative medicine and treatments are sufficiently dangerous that, in order to benefit from them, we have to be constantly on our guard against their excesses. These excesses include the hubris of thinking we can keep ourselves free from disease by carefully controlling our diet and the disregard of common sense that suggests severely restricting what you eat is healthy. These excesses may not be typical of alternative medicine, but they certainly do exist. We need to guard against these as much as we do against the excesses of science. Similar points can be made about the dangers of free markets, government regulations, exercise, and civil defence.

But the real sting comes from the fact that science is essential to protect us from its own dangers. For example, new drugs never come without risks. It is hopelessly optimistic to expect that we can develop new treatments for serious diseases without running the risk that some will have harmful side effects. If we want the benefits of these new drugs, we therefore have to take risks. And the best way to minimize these risks is to ensure rigorous scientific testing. So it may be true that science needs to be kept in check, but part of that checking process must itself be scientific.

It is obvious that much harm has been caused by the misuse of scientific knowledge. What I have argued is that this does not justify an anti-scientific attitude. First, the fact that scientific knowledge has been misused is not necessarily a criticism of scientists, but of those who use their findings. Second, science itself is essential to the monitoring and controlling of the possible harms that can be caused by the application of scientific knowledge. And it also needs to be remembered that science is the cause of much good. Many people walking around today—maybe even you—owe their lives to the fact that scientific advances have enabled them to survive what would once have been fatal. Sitting in an insalubrious but comfortable room, with heating, a computer, a telephone, a fridge, and water on tap, I would feel a fraud decrying science, which lies behind the technologies that make all of these things possible. Many harms do have their roots in science, but many good things grow from the same soil.

Playing God

Whatever the actual harms caused by science, many are made uneasy when the frontiers of science start extending into previously unexplored territory. This is particularly evident in the objections raised to human therapeutic cloning. Here, the phrase we often hear used is 'scientists playing God'. Like many catchy slogans, when you come to unpack what precisely it means, you find it doesn't mean any one clear thing at all. Rather, the phrase captures a variety of doubts and anxieties, many of which are vague, and articulates them in a rhetorically powerful way.

Nevertheless, this is no reason to dismiss the objection out of hand. Often legitimate concerns are voiced in ways which, if subjected to close scrutiny, can seem obscure, muddled, or silly.

If our enquiry is to be earnest, we need to invoke the principle of charity, which states that one should always examine the strongest or most plausible interpretation of the ideas one is examining. Otherwise, we would merely be examining a particular, perhaps weak, articulation of an idea, not the idea itself.

So what can the idea of 'playing God' plausibly mean? Sometimes this phrase is used to express the idea that there is something wrong with 'tampering with nature' or doing something 'unnatural'. These ideas are examined in the next chapter, on the environment. Another interpretation is that scientists lack the authority to extend their techniques into certain areas of life, which are 'no-go areas'. One can believe this whether or not one believes in the existence of the God scientists are accused of trying to supplant. For example, a convinced atheist will almost always believe that scientists lack the authority to conduct certain forms of experiment, such as those which require causing pain to adults against their wishes. In the case of human cloning, it might be argued that this is such a case of scientists exceeding their authority. Put another way, they have no *right* to use human life in this way.

This argument rests partly on a proper understanding of what is meant by authority. In broad terms, authority is legitimate power. A person or institution has the authority to do something if it has been empowered by a legitimate means to do so. This definition invites further questions, such as what constitutes legitimacy. As is often the case, however, we don't need to answer all the questions raised by a problem in order to make progress with it. In this instance, this is because we can broadly agree about what kinds of things scientists have the authority to do. People do disagree about the authority scientists have to experiment on humans. They also disagree about the authority scientists have to alter nature, which as I have said is discussed in the next chapter. But almost everyone would agree, I think, that scientists do not have the authority to engage in any kind of experiment which harms human life or creates unacceptable risks for humans. And we would none of us think they lacked the authority to experiment on inert substances such as rocks and atoms, unless that had the effect of harming humans or, depending on your view, animals. When we agree on so much that is necessary to move forward on an issue, there is simply no point in trying to resolve all remaining disagreements first.

In the case of human cloning, therefore, setting aside the 'tampering with nature' question, the other bone of contention is the scientists' authority to harm human life. The morality of ending human life is something I will come to in more detail in Chapter 9. For now I will merely assume what I later argue for, namely that there is no reason to place a special protection on all life in the biological line *homo sapiens*. Rather, it is *persons* we think of as special: persons roughly being individuals with a sense of self, capable of thought and feeling. Almost all humans are persons and there may be no persons that are not humans, but it is not being human which makes someone a person. We say harming human life is wrong, but we should really say harming persons is wrong. And we have to remember that human therapeutic cloning is about using cells from early embryos, which are immature exemplars of the species *homo sapiens* but should not be considered persons.

There are other ways that such experiments could harm persons. If the consequence of this cloning is that we produce 'monsters' or reduce the genetic diversity of the population, then human therapeutic cloning would harm persons, not because the experiments are on persons, but because of their effects on humans. However, there is simply no reason to believe these doomsday scenarios. Indeed, the aim of human therapeutic cloning is to find cures to human diseases, not to start factory lines of identical cloned people or variations on Frankenstein's monster. So if by 'playing God' we mean that scientists are going beyond their authority and harming persons, the accusation just doesn't stand, in this instance and in countless others where scientists are criticized. The only no-go areas are those which make things worse.

The idea of scientists playing God may also be linked with the fear of social engineering. We do not want the future to be a world in which human freedom and individuality has been sacrificed so that scientists can create a 'better', perfected version of humanity. Such a dystopia is presented in the film *Gattaca*, where people are divided between those whose parents made sure they had a 'superior' genetic make-up and those who were conceived the old-fashioned way. In such a future, scientists are not so much playing God but playing a combination of deity and dictator.

These concerns are legitimate, though often exaggerated. The point is that there is nothing in the science itself which makes such a future necessary. This returns us to the point made earlier about science and its uses. One can only create this kind of dystopia if governments make it happen. Given the great resistance in the population to this kind of future, that does not seem likely to happen. What we need to fear is malevolent dictatorship, not science. A malevolent (or misguided) dictatorship will use whatever materials are to hand to limit freedom and individual liberty. The fact that they could use genetic technologies to achieve this is no more an argument against genetics than the fact that they could use the police to do it is an argument against having a police force.

So—deferring for a moment the question of the right to tamper with nature—nothing we have seen so far justifies the claim that human therapeutic cloning is an instance of scientists playing God. As long as experiments, research, and the use of its findings is properly used, we need have no fear that people will be harmed, either directly or by deleterious effects on society.

Unreliable science

The third accusation is that we are constantly been asked to trust in science even though its findings are unreliable and often contradictory. You often hear people complaining that scientists are telling us one thing one minute and something completely different the next. This is one reason why some people refuse to take dietary advice seriously. Here there is a connection between our two case studies: the alleged fact that scientists had got it very wrong with BSE is used as evidence that we should not trust their reassuring words about human therapeutic cloning. No risk to human life? Where have we heard that one before?

The problem here seems to be a misunderstanding of what science can and cannot do. In one respect this is a controversial issue. For example, there is wide disagreement amongst philosophers of science about just what scientific method is and what kind of truth or reality science describes. But for scientists themselves, these disputes are largely irrelevant: science is something they just do. The British biologist Lewis Wolpert speaks for many in the scientific community when he repeatedly complains the philosophy of science has added nothing to scientists' understanding of their enterprise. The claim is surely exaggerated, but not without foundation.

Despite these controversies, there is still enough agreement about the status of scientific findings to answer critics who complain it is unreliable. The short answer is, if you mean by 'unreliable' that scientific findings do not always turn out to be right, then it is true that science is unreliable. The problem here is not the unreliability, however, but the failure to take account of this unreliability. Take as an example a health story that filled many news pages over several years in Britain: the possibility that the combined measles, mumps, and rubella (MMR) vaccine could cause serious health problems in children. A few small scientific studies, including one by Andrew Wakefield of London's Royal Free Hospital, suggested the combined MMR vaccine could cause autism and Crohn's disease, a serious bowel disorder. But against this, other evidence suggested there was no such link. This evidence includes a Finnish study which followed two million children for fourteen years and found no heath risks. In any case, the alternative is to administer the vaccines separately, but because this has to be done over an extended period of time, children are left vulnerable to infection for longer. So any reduction in the, at worst, small risk of MMR side effects would be more than offset by greater risks of actually catching the diseases being vaccinated against.

What we have here then is a classic case where there is no conclusive proof on either side, only a balance of evidence to be weighed up and the best hypothesis formed. How precisely this is done is a big controversy in the philosophy of science. But in general terms, there is agreement that the general form of such reasoning is inductive: that is to say, there are no logically watertight proofs, only fallible reasoning from experience. In the jargon, this means that any scientific claim is defeasible, meaning it is in principle open to revision or rejection in the light of further disclosures, arguments, or evidence.

In the MMR case, however, people do not want to hear about defeasibility and inductive probability. What they want to know is whether the vaccine is safe or not. If the health authorities sound too cagey then this causes widespread concern. So these agencies tend to play by the public's rules and say that the vaccine is safe, period, glossing over the fact that any such judgement is fallible and could be wrong.

The nature of the news media does not help. While scientists know that the best way to get it right is to look across all studies that have taken place on a particular subject, the news media thrives on highlighting the 'latest' or most interesting study. So, you get a sequence of headlines such as these from the British quality daily, the *Independent*:

Study claims MMR vaccine trials were inadequate (21 January 2001)

MMR vaccine not linked to autism, researchers claim (10 February 2001)

MMR vaccine is linked to bleeding disorder, says government adviser (22 February 2001)

One jab good, three jabs bad (21 August 2001)

Children at risk of seizures just after MMR jab (30 August 2001)

Scientists discount link between MMR vaccine and autism (13 December 2001)

New MMR fears over measles link to bowel disease (6 February 2002)

This creates an impression that scientists keep changing their minds about whether the MMR vaccine is safe. But what is really happening is that each individual study is just one more piece of evidence. 'Scientific opinion', to the extent that it is monolithic at all, is based on considering what all these studies together suggest, not on what one appears to show.

So it is wrong to say that scientists can't make up their minds about the safety of the MMR vaccine and give conflicting advice. Rather, most scientists agree that the balance of evidence suggests that it is safe and that even if there are associated risks, these risks are worth taking, because the alternatives are riskier.

Another important consequence of the way in which scientific opinion develops is that, at any given time, several theories which are generally believed to be right will turn out to be wrong. This is just inevitable. A fallible source of knowledge, which is what science is, is going to make mistakes. When we see these mistakes, as perhaps we did in the BSE crisis (though remember it is politicians and civil servants rather than scientists who were most blamed by the official report), our 'faith in science' is weakened. But only if we expect science to be able to deliver us certainties will we be shocked when some of its findings turn out to be false.

At the beginning of this chapter I mentioned the curious fact that science is, in some instances, considered the highest authority and yet, in others, utterly distrusted and blamed for many of our ills. Perhaps what we have just looked at explains the link. We think that science should be the source of certain knowledge, perhaps the most certain that we can obtain. A MORI poll published in 2002, for example, found that 71 per cent of the British public expect all scientists to agree about scientific issues and 61 per cent expect science to provide 100 per cent safety guarantees on medicines. Thus we put science on a pedestal—our highest human achievement. Then science gets something wrong and we find our idol has feet of clay. The answer is to be realistic in the first place. If we understand what kind of knowledge science is capable of producing—the best possible evidence-based accounts, but inductive, fallible, and defeasible, rather than certain and infallible—we will be in a better position to judge how to react to its findings.

An end to wonder?

Often when we don't like something and we're asked why, we give reasons which, in reality, are not the real explanation at all. This is often not deliberate deceit. Rather, feeling the need to give a reason, we invent one on the spot and kid ourselves we believe it. So, I don't find a popular television series funny, someone asks me why not, and I find myself saying, and believing, 'the characters are so unbelievable'. Yet if I thought about it I'd soon realize that my favourite comedies also feature unbelievable characters. This can't be the reason why I don't find it funny.

Similarly, people might say that science is at the root of too much harm, that it is unreliable, and that scientists shouldn't play God. But perhaps their anti-science attitude is motivated by something quite different. One such motivation might be a feeling that the scientific approach to life is too reductive—that it makes the world a mere lump of matter and us mere machines. Love, truth, and beauty have no place in the scientific worldview and so such a view needs to be resisted.

This is pertinent to the case of human cloning. Here a fear seems to be that science is attempting to plumb the mystery of the self. We feel that our essence as individuals is something that cannot be reduced to a string of genetic code. The fear is that by cloning humans, science is laying claim to the essentially mysterious and private core of our being. We cease to become irreducible, whole selves, and are converted instead into manufacturable human 'products'.

To address this concern about science requires us to consider what it means to call an explanation reductive. An explanation is reductive if it explains one phenomenon in terms of other, more basic ones. So, for example, a reductive explanation of rainbows explains the visible phenomenon of the spectrum arc in terms of the more basic facts about light, particles, and refraction. These are considered more basic because they do all the causal work in the explanation. The existence of the rainbow is explained by reduction to light, particles, and refraction. They tell us what causes what we see.

Reductive explanations are the bread and butter of science and lie behind its huge success. Most of the time, they pose no threat to our everyday beliefs. Knowing what causes rainbows in no way detracts from enjoying them, a point made in scientist Richard Dawkins's book, *Unweaving the Rainbow*. Nor have I heard of a musician whose enjoyment of music is lessened by knowledge that sound is vibration of the air. However, on other occasions people feel a very strong gut resistance to reductionist explanations, especially when they refer to personality. We hate to think that the reason we are the way we are is because of our genes, for example. We instinctively feel that we are not just strings of DNA. And though musicians may be happy to accept sound is air vibrating, they become very agitated when it is suggested that we can explain why certain pieces of music are more enjoyable than others in terms of how they affect the brain. In both examples, the plea seems to be, you can explain only so much by reduction, but there are certain spheres of human life which cannot be explained in this way.

This response is one part unnecessary and one part debatable. If you start with the unnecessary, reductive explanations are a lot less of a threat than they often seem. Take a simple example of wine. What if it were possible for a team of scientists to analyse the different elements that go up to make the flavour of a wine and then be able to predict the taste and quality of a wine without it touching their lips? And what if they were also to explain why some flavours are more pleasurable than others, because they could trace the links between the pleasure-sensing areas of the brain and the effects of the different elements on the taste buds? Such research would be fascinating, though a dubious use of resources. But it would certainly do nothing to eliminate the pleasure of drinking the wine. More significantly, it would not render the wine taster's descriptions of wine redundant. A chemical description of the wine would not help me choose a bottle in the supermarket, but knowing it is full-bodied and oaky with a hint of cherry may well do so. So the reductive explanation threatens neither the way in which we enjoy wine nor the way in which we talk about it. Reductionism has limits in the sense that there will always be countless situations where the reductionist explanation is simply inappropriate to our needs. Even if the whole world could be explained in reductionist terms, we wouldn't actually use these explanations in our everyday discourse. We still talk of the sunrise, for example, even though we know the sun isn't rising at all.

In the same way, the fact that you can 'reduce' an individual human being to a string of genetic code does not at all eliminate the whole self. Indeed, the genetic code is no more than a 'blueprint'. What an individual actually becomes depends upon how they go through and respond to life. It is therefore especially misplaced to think that human cloning threatens the idea of the self because the self can never be contained within our genes alone. If it could, then all that we are, will, and have been would be present at the moment of conception. As it is, at that point the self, as a conscious, feeling, thinking entity has not even begun to exist. This shows that it is wrong to see genes as being the reductive explanation of the self. Whereas all that the rainbow is can be explained by the account of the refraction of light, not all that the self is can be explained in terms of genes. Our genes are only part of the story of who we are.

A less philosophical, but real, worry is that once a reduction has been made, we become redundant. For instance, while it may be true the wine taster's vocabulary is not made redundant by our imaginary tasting machine, the wine taster herself may be. Maybe the scientists could get so good at their job that they could programme a computer to be a wine critic. For this to be a real success, the programme would have also to be witty and inventive in its use of language.

With cloning perhaps we fear that parenting will become redundant, since we will end up creating children in laboratories. Such possibilities are at the very best a long way off and may be impossible. Part of the worry of all this is an understandable Luddite fear that technology will make us all useless. In the short term technology can take away people's roles or work. But in the long run humanity finds more things to do for itself after technology has taken away a burden. And though we might imagine the wine-tasting machine taking over someone's job, the parental drive is such a strong human instinct that there seems no reason to suppose technology will get in the way of it. Methods of conception may change, but since most sex is not undertaken for reproduction, it is hard to see why anyone would lament that fact. In any case, our concern here is with human therapeutic cloning and this not an alternative method of procreation.

So the fear of being made useless is probably overstated and the fear of a loss of our everyday pleasures and ways of seeing and talking about the world largely unfounded. Nevertheless, a fear remains and at the heart of that fear is the idea that if everything can be explained in reductive terms, we are somehow less than what we think ourselves to be. We think of ourselves as unique, free individuals who use our feelings and our minds to find our way through this world. But if our feelings, thoughts, and individuality are all explained, not by genes alone, but by genes, brain processes, and our interaction with the world, then are we not more like machines than men? This, we feel, is intolerable.

The problem with this response is that what is intolerable may well be true. Should we then despair? I don't think so. Knowing something is true on one level of explanation does not automatically wipe away what we perceive to be true on another. The fact that thought processes can be described in terms of brain processes does not mean the thought processes do not go on, just as the reductionist explanation of rainbows does not show rainbows don't exist. We don't need to stop saying we're depressed and say our serotonin is low instead. Our common-sense view of the world is here to stay for it is too ingrained to go away. Reductionist explanations needn't threaten them.

It would, however, be disingenuous to pretend that everything in a reduced world will be comfortable to accept. The extent to which we are free, for example, may have to be revised if we accept reductionist explanations of behaviour. It might just be the case that all our actions and beliefs are fundamentally explained by the workings of brain chemicals over which we have no control. That would be, I think, hard to accept. But the consequences need not be all bad. I would guess that on average, people who believe we are absolutely free are more likely to be retributive and vindictive and less likely to be understanding of other people's deficiencies than those who believe we do not have free will. On this score, I'd rather we had more people not believing in free will than believing in it.

So the fear of a too-reductive science can be lessened by several considerations. First, reductive explanations, where they are available, are not appropriate for all types of discourse. The language of the wine taster is more useful for us than the language of the lab. Second, accepting a reductionist explanation need not diminish our enjoyment of the world and all that is in it. Finally, even if everything, including our very human nature, can be explained in reductive terms, we will not stop experiencing life as we currently do. We will feel free, decision-making will to us still depend on thought, and so on. The sun still rises for Copernicus.

Conclusion

As BSE and human therapeutic cloning show, science can fail us and science can scare us. This is no reason, however, to turn against science. Harm can come from science, that is certain. But so can good and more often than not it is society, not scientists, who are able to determine which of these outcomes prevails. Whether human cloning is used for good or bad is for us to decide. How the government used scientific advice during the BSE saga was the responsibility of government, not scientists. Science extends the frontiers of human possibilities, even giving us control over the conception of human beings. But to say this is 'playing God' is to make an accusation that cannot be sustained. Science is fallible, but that will only be seen as disgraceful by those who fail to understand some basic philosophical points about the limits of scientific knowledge. Science is reductive, but that does not make a painting less beautiful or us less human.

We need to see through the hyperbole of both advocates and critics of science and I think philosophy can help us do that. Philosophy at its best nurtures a healthy, non-destructive scepticism, and this kind of attitude towards science will serve to protect us against the excesses of scientism much more than a wholesale anti-scientific outlook. We should neither accept easy reassurances backed up by scientific findings nor hysterical scare stories which latch onto individual pieces of research. We will only be able to assess the claims of science with a clear mind if we lose the fear and loathing which too often leads to a knee-jerk rejection of scientific advances.

6

Green thinking: Conceptualizing the environment

Genetically modified foods

On 26 July 1999, twenty-eight members of the environmental group Greenpeace entered Walnut Tree Farm in Norfolk, England and began shredding and bagging a six-acre crop of maize. This maize was genetically modified (GM) and was being grown on the farm as part of a trial. Farmers fought off the activists, using tractors. The activists, including the former government minister Lord Melchett, were taken to court for causing criminal damage. But on 20 September 2000, a Norwich jury cleared them all of the charges.

The acquittal meant that further cases against other protestors were brought on the charge of aggravated trespass, rather than criminal damage. But when on 16 October 2001 the high court cleared another group of activists of this charge, it seemed that this legal route was also futile. The protestors have all, so far, escaped punishment in the law courts.

Intriguingly, how we view this story might depend on where we live. GM foods are a major consumer concern in the UK, but not in the USA. So one question is whether the British are paranoid or the Americans are complacent. A more directly relevant question is whether we should be applauding the success of the plucky activists against agribusiness's rape of nature or lamenting the fact that a group of vandals has gone unpunished. How we answer this question depends largely on whether we think the environmentalists are right to perceive the planting of GM crops as irresponsible and dangerous. Philosophy has a role to play here, but we need to be clear about the scope and limits of this role.

We could take as our model the philosopher Janet Radcliffe

Richards's exemplary book *The Sceptical Feminist* (1980). In it, she examined the kinds of arguments heard to support and attack feminist positions. She was not concerned with the more obscure ends of feminist theory but with the feminist arguments that had a wider currency. The result was a book which supported the feminist cause, but rejected many of the weaker arguments put forward in its favour.

A similar book could be published on the environment. In 2001, a book did come out with the title of *The Skeptical Environmentalist*, but this was very different in that it involved an exhaustive and exhausting examination of the many statistics and facts used in evidence by the environmental lobby. The book probably holds the record for the largest number of footnotes in a popular paperback.[1] There can be no doubt that a proper consideration of environmental issues does require us to consider a wide range of facts. This is, of course, not a philosophical enterprise. But there is, in parallel to this, a contribution philosophy can make to the debate. This contribution could follow Radcliffe Richards's model. What philosophers can do is examine those arguments made by the environmental lobby which do not rest on contended facts, but on questions of value, principle, and logic. These arguments are often more effective than those that rest on facts anyway. For instance, a poll conducted by the *Independent on Sunday* in February 1999 found 68 per cent of people were afraid of eating GM foods. Since it is certain that less than 68 per cent of people understand the science behind GM foods, it cannot be the facts that are motivating this fear.

[1] This book only has one.

So what I intend to do here is provide a kind of précis of the book I wish Radcliffe Richards would write on the environment. This would not be the last word on the issue, because we need facts and information to come to a final verdict. But at the very least we should be able to clear the conceptual ground so that the examination of the facts can be conducted in a clear and intelligent way.

What are GM foods?

To begin with, we need to get clear about what GM foods are and why they are contentious. Since one opinion poll showed that many people thought that only GM foods contained genes at all, more informed readers will forgive me if I proceed quite carefully here.

All living things contain genes. Each cell of a living thing contains chromosomes, which are formed of sequences of DNA (deoxyribonucleic acid) which contain the information required for the cell to 'build' the organism it is part of. The exact definition of a gene is technical, but for our purposes, all we need to know is that it comprises a specific sequence of nucleotides in DNA. Genetic information is inherited and sexual reproduction always results in a new mix of genes.

In nature and in traditional farming, cross-breeding takes place, in which genes become mixed to produce new varieties of plants and new breeds of animals. However, now it is possible for scientists to do this mixing in the laboratory. This makes new kinds of mixing possible. For example, in nature, one could never mix genes from a carrot with those of a pig. Now we can.

The point of making such genetic modifications to food and livestock is to produce new breeds and varieties that improve on what nature has provided. So, for example, we could make wheat which is hardier and drought-resistant; tomatoes that stay ripe for longer; rice that contains higher levels of vitamins and minerals; potatoes that resist pests without the need for pesticides, and so on. Of course, we could also make frivolous things, such as green carrots or cocoa-flavoured coffee beans.

So why do some oppose GM foods? There are several reasons. Some argue that we do not know how safe these foods will be for humans. Others argue that allowing these new crops into the environment will unsettle the natural balance and reduce biodiversity, by overtaking traditional varieties. This will harm the environment, perhaps irrevocably. Some express the concern that we should not tamper with nature or that it is wrong to do what is so unnatural. Others worry that agribusinesses will abuse the power they will have by their ownership of these new varieties by forcing farmers in the developing world to pay high prices for new batches of seed every year.

Here I will address only those concerns that have a philosophical component. For example, the question of the threat to human health is a medical and scientific matter, not a philosophical one. The question of whether it is possible or wrong to harm the environment is, however, one for philosophy, for there is a conceptual problem about how an unconscious thing can be said to be harmed.

Tampering with nature

In the previous chapter I considered the question of whether scientists play God, and many of those considerations also apply here. To recap, there was no specific kind of scientific activity which could properly be classified as 'playing God' and so the real issue concerned whether science caused harm. Similarly, the accusation that we play God with nature will usually also boil down to the claim that we cause harm to the natural environment, and the specific idea of 'playing God' will fall away. I will look more at what it means to harm nature later.

One issue held over from the last chapter was the idea that it is wrong to tamper with nature. Another very similar idea is that it is wrong to do what is unnatural. Both claims are often implied in arguments, but rarely made explicit. Perhaps the reason for this is that, once made explicit, their weaknesses become evident.

The idea that it is wrong to 'tamper with nature' is, at least in its unsophisticated forms, pretty absurd. The first question has to be, what counts as tampering with nature? A beaver builds a dam and changes the river flow. Is it therefore an environmental terrorist? Of course not. But what if we build dams to generate electricity or protect low-lying regions from floods? Often such schemes are criticized for 'tampering with nature' or 'interfering with the ecosystem'. But so do beaver dams.

The obvious reply is that the beaver is acting out of instinct and its dam-building has a role to play in the ecosystem which has gradually evolved over millions of years. Human dam-building, on the other hand, is a massive intrusion that will totally alter the ecosystem. In other words, the beaver's dam is in harmony with nature, the human's dam is in conflict with it.

The reply is highly instructive, for if you look at it carefully it does not amount to the claim that tampering with nature is wrong. Both beavers and humans tamper with nature. The difference between humans and the beaver is that human tampering is on a larger and more destructive scale. It is not the tampering per se that is considered wrong, it is the effects of that tampering. This is an important point to acknowledge, because the claim that it is wrong to alter nature is made very frequently. Beavers fell trees, elephants trample plants, ants strip trees of bark, moles dig tunnels, and so the list goes on. There isn't a living thing which doesn't alter its natural environment in some way. In the long run that can lead to changes in landscape, foliage, and animal populations. It also leads to extinction of some species. None of these things is considered wrong. But when humans do the same, we accuse ourselves of 'tampering with nature'. That in itself is surely not a bad thing. It can only be bad for some other reason. If our tampering is wrong, it must be the specific nature or scale of it which makes it wrong.

We are moving towards a more refined understanding of the claim that we should not interfere with nature. The idea now is that such interference is a bad thing when it is used to make large-scale or damaging changes to nature. But this too seems suspicious. Why should the mere scale of the change make it a bad thing? If making small changes to nature is not wrong, why should making large changes be such a bad thing? Take this thought experiment. Many people believe it is right to try to protect endangered species from extinction. Imagine that at some time in the future, an international body is set up to monitor the populations of millions of plants and animals around the world. As soon as the population of any plant or animal reaches a dangerously low point, they intervene to protect it from its predators and to help it return to a stable population. If this project is carried out on a large scale, it will add up to a massive amount of human alteration of the course of nature. Though no doubt some of this will be to 'correct' damage previously done by humans, a great deal will not. Would such a massive alteration of nature be a bad thing? There are many reasons to think it would be, but none of them is solely to do with the scale of the operation. It seems to me that if you believe protecting endangered species is a good thing, there is no particular reason why massive intervention to protect endangered species should be a bad thing just because of its scale. Indeed, many would think the opposite—that because saving species from extinction is a good thing a huge operation to do so would be very good indeed.

So the defence shifts again. Now it seems we are wrong to tamper with nature only in so far as it is harmful to do so. It is not tampering per se which is wrong, nor its scale, but the nature of the tampering. Of course, it may be the case that large-scale tampering tends to cause more harm than small-scale tampering, but that does not show that it is the scale in itself which is wrong.

This seems a perfectly reasonable position. After all, isn't it moral to be against anything that causes more harm than good? Of course it is, but what we have to notice is that we have ended up with a principle which is nothing specifically to do with nature at all. The idea that we should not do anything which causes harm is a general principle of morality and not a specific criticism of 'tampering with nature' at all. The grounds of the objection could apply to any human activity. If one agrees with it, one would also, for example, have to be against those aspects of rugby which, on balance, result in harm (if indeed there are any such aspects). If interfering with nature is morally wrong at all, it is because it causes harm, not because 'interfering with nature' is a specifically bad form of behaviour.

The implications for our attitudes to GM foods are thus clear. If we are wrong to press ahead with the development of GM foods it must be because we judge that it is dangerous and harmful to do so, or that the risks are not outweighed by the potential benefits. The idea that it is wrong because it is 'tampering with nature' is thus a red herring. Only harmful tampering is wrong, so GM foods should only be opposed if it is actually harmful or if the risks of it causing harm are sufficiently high. There are, of course, arguments on either side here. One problem with assessing them is that people are increasingly distrustful of science and it is science which is the best source of reliable information about the risks. Hopefully what I said in the previous chapter should address some of those concerns. It is of course harder to assess the facts about GM foods than it is simply to apply some general principle about it being wrong to meddle with nature, but then responding intelligently to current affairs is difficult. That is why we (and philosophers are not immune to this vice) often prefer to shout at the television or tut-tut at the newspaper rather than really think about what lies behind what is being said.

The natural and the good

The philosophical roots of this error are more evident if we consider the similar argument that what is natural is somehow good and what is unnatural bad. Again, the principle is rarely stated so explicitly, but if we look at what people actually do, this does seem to be an assumption that underlies people's behaviour. Consider, for example, the popularity of 'natural' remedies. A great many people would always prefer to take a 'natural' remedy over an 'artificial' one. Similarly, people prefer foods that have 'all natural' ingredients.

One obvious point to make here is that this very characterization of certain things as 'natural' is problematic. What always strikes me about health food shops are the rows and rows of bottles and tablets. A greengrocer seems to be a much better source of natural products than such collections of distilled essences and the like. There is also a question about why people suppose natural remedies are better for them or carry fewer risks. For a remedy to work, it must affect one's body. And if it affects one's body, it is always possible, especially if testing has not been extensive, that it will affect it adversely. What is more, many 'natural' remedies have not been tested. Hence it is no surprise if it turns out, with extensive testing, that a treatment like St John's Wort—generally safe and probably effective against mild depression—can have negative as well as positive effects. The only things we can guarantee as safe are those which do not affect us at all, and these, of course, cannot remedy anything either.

However, let us set aside such doubts about the category of 'the natural' for the moment and just ask, even if we can agree that some things are natural and some are not, what follows from this? The answer is: nothing. It is certainly nothing from the point of view of fact. There is no factual reason to suppose that what is natural is good (or at least better) and what is unnatural is bad (or at least worse). A striking example is water supply. Clean water is perhaps the single most important thing to improve the life chances of people in the developing world. When communities rely on 'natural' sources, they expose themselves to disease. At the very least, they need unnatural apparatus, such as pumps, to access clean water supplies. And in many cases, we need the full, unnatural apparatus of a chlorinated mains water supply to meet everyone's needs. Anyone who suggests we would do better to go back to nature for our water supply is frankly nuts.

Of course, there are many particular instances where what is natural is better. A diet rich in wholegrains and vegetables is healthier than one rich in processed food, for example. But there is no general principle that says natural is always better. We need to consider each case on its merits. Even in the example of diet, it is clear that the healthiest diet requires some intervention of the unnatural. We can get a better, healthier diet—especially in places such as northern Europe—when we can import vegetables during the winter, grow others in greenhouses, keep things refrigerated, pasteurize milk, and so on. A purely 'natural' diet—one which relied on locally produced, untreated produce alone—would see us severely limited in what we could eat, and less healthy as a result.

So the facts should not lead us to think that the natural is good. Logic in this case confirms what we should know by experience by showing us that no statements concerning values such as 'good' can follow from statements that are purely about facts such as what is 'natural'. Hume was perhaps the first philosopher to make the point that there is a distinction between statements of fact and statements of value. To say something *is* the case is always different from saying that it *ought to be* the case. This is why Hume's principle has become known as the is/ought gap, or the fact/value distinction. The logical point is that, because there is this difference, one can never infer from a simple statement of fact any statement of value. So, for example, it does not follow from the fact that spanking causes pain (a statement of fact) that spanking is morally wrong (a statement of value). Of course, we can invoke the fact that spanking causes pain as evidence that it is wrong, but in order to reach the conclusion that it is wrong, we need an evaluative premise such as 'causing pain is wrong'. Such evaluative premises are never themselves matters of fact; rather they are matters of judgement. This confirms the point that matters of fact alone are never enough to establish matters of value.

This distinction has come under some criticism by professional philosophers recently, but, at the very least, it is still generally accepted that there is no *direct* or *immediate* means of establishing a matter of value from a matter of fact. How does this impact on the question of the natural? The point here is that to say something is natural is only to state a fact. But if facts are distinct from values, it can never be inferred from the mere fact that something is natural that it is good, or from the mere fact that it is unnatural that it is bad. 'This is natural' does not tell us if this is good or bad.

This again has obvious implications for the GM food debate. People do not like the idea that GM food is unnatural. But it does not follow from the fact that it is unnatural that it is bad. In fact, like chlorinated water, it may turn out that this is something unnatural and good. So, again, what settles the matter are facts. Whether or not GM foods are good or bad depends on the facts about them. Although much of the debate about GM foods invokes facts, one can't escape the feeling that a lot of the time people are looking for the facts that support their intuitive sense that GM foods are unnatural and therefore bad. There is not much impartial consideration of what all the facts together suggest. Philosophy's role here is to remove the fallacy that connects the natural with what is good so that the facts can be considered in an appropriately dispassionate way.

Value-laden language

There is an important rhetorical feature of the discourse about environmentalism which gets in the way of clear thought. Rhetoric is usually contrasted with argument proper in that the goal of rhetoric is to persuade by any available means, whereas the point of argument is to come up with rationally sound arguments. In reality, the distinction is not so clear. Since Plato's attacks on the sophists, who would present persuasive arguments to support whoever would pay them to do so, philosophers have supposedly eschewed rhetoric. But in many philosophical papers and books you will find examples of it at work. Similarly, sometimes a good argument can also be very persuasive, so something can be both a good argument and a good piece of rhetoric.

Our interest is in those cases where rhetoric and good argument clearly come apart. In these cases, people use words in order to make their case more appealing, but there is no substance to the arguments they appear to be putting forward. A blatant example of rhetoric is when someone talks about doing something 'for the sake of our children' without giving any evidence or argument that what they want to do is in the best interests of children. In a good (from a rhetorical point of view) speech or article, the absence of the argument or evidence goes unnoticed.

The rhetorical feature of the environmental debate I want to focus on is the way in which the very words which are used to describe the issues themselves have evaluative connotations. We can see this when environmental protestors are called 'eco-terrorists' or 'vandals'. But it is the environmentalists who have been most successful in getting the debate framed in words that suit them. For example, on 17 October 2001, the *Guardian* newspaper, reporting the acquittal of the Greenpeace activists, said: 'The jury accepted the Greenpeace defence that criminal damage was justified if it was used to defend a greater public interest, namely preventing the contamination of the environment by genetically modified organisms.'

Here, the key word is 'contamination'. This is clearly a word with negative connotations. If one were to ask people whether they approved of contaminating the countryside with GM crops, most would answer no, purely because it is hard to see how contamination could ever be good. But what does contamination actually mean in this situation? What it means is that there would be a cross-pollination of the GM crops with neighbouring crops. Cross-pollination occurs all the time in nature, so to say all cross-pollination is contamination is to twist language by using a negative word to describe what is normally neither good nor bad. So one can only justify using this term if one already believes that such cross-pollination is harmful. But, of course, this is precisely what is being contested. So, the environmentalists have scored a huge rhetorical success here. They have succeeded in establishing the word 'contamination' as the usual term for cross-pollination between GM and non-GM crops. Such is their success that major national news media use the word in what is supposed to be a purely factual account. Yet that 'factual account' masks a partial evaluation, which has been smuggled in.

In the battle for hearts and minds, this linguistic front is vital. In an article written after the court case, Lord Melchett used the phrase 'genetic pollution' as another value-laden way of describing cross-pollination between GM and non-GM crops. It is important to the campaigners that such phrases get adopted. Other such words have already established themselves in the environmental discourse. 'Exploitation' is one. All creatures, humans, beavers, birds, and flies make use of their environment. They adapt it to suit their needs. One could say that they exploit the environment, and there is a perfectly acceptable sense of the word 'exploit' which does not carry with it any negative connotations. But, as a matter of fact, we tend to use the word 'exploit' in situations where someone makes use of something inappropriately. So the word does have a negative connotation. This means that environmentalists can talk about humans exploiting the environment as if they were describing simple facts, while at the same time loading into the description a negative judgement.

There are countless other examples of this, some more obvious than others. Some get quite complex. Consider the simple phrase 'disturbing the natural balance'. Here, we have two words, 'nature' and 'balance', which carry with them positive connotations, set against the negative 'disturb'. Yet this has become such a natural way of speaking (natural does not necessarily mean good, of course) that attempts to describe it in more neutral terms can sound artificial: 'altering the existing distribution of organisms in the world' just doesn't have the same ring.

When the very words we use to report and discuss environmental news stories carry these evaluative connotations, moving beyond rhetoric to serous argument becomes even more difficult. Yet we must make this effort, or else we risk being blinded by language to the truth that language purports to represent. If we want to know whether GM foods are good or bad, we hardly start our enquiry on an impartial basis if we describe things that may or may not be bad as pollution or contamination.

Harming the environment

Perhaps the best example of how values slip into ordinary discourse comes in simple expressions such as 'harming' or 'damaging' the environment. In the GM foods debate, the supposed harm that GM foods threaten is biodiversity. (Human health is not actually considered a serious risk by most informed commentators, even though the public identifies it as a major concern.) There seems to be nothing objectionable or value-laden in such phrases. To the extent that they carry judgements—harm and damage are negative, of course—these judgements are explicit, not concealed. We only say we harm the environment in contexts when the environment is actually harmed, don't we?

The problem here is with the conceptualization of the environment. In order to make sense of the claim that the environment is harmed we have to have an idea of the environment as something which can be harmed or helped. Normally the kinds of things which we think can be harmed or helped are those things for which things can be going better or worse. With human beings, we have a pretty good idea of what it means for things to go better or worse for them. Crudely, if we're healthy and happy, things are going well; if we're sick and miserable, they're going badly. In contrast, the idea that things can go well or badly for a rock just doesn't seem to make sense. It would be a kind of parody of the idea of respect for nature to say, for example, that things are going well for a rock when it stands proudly on a precipice and badly when it tumbles and shatters.

What the contrast suggests is that the paradigmatic idea of things going well or badly requires a point of view from which things can appear better or worse. Things can go well or badly for a human because a human has a point of view which enables him or her to judge or feel that things are good or bad. The rock lacks such a point of view and so things cannot go well or badly for it. This point of view can be variously described as subjectivity or consciousness.

The problem with the environment is that it has no point of view. In Thomas Nagel's terminology, there is *nothing it is like* to be a planet or 'the environment'. But if the environment lacks this point of view, this subjectivity, in what way does it make sense to say that things can go well or badly for it?

At this point it is worth briefly mentioning a mode of thought which would reject the path my argument is taking. So-called 'deep-greens' would argue that the planet is rather like or actually is an organism with a point of view from which things can go better or worse. This outlook is rooted in the Gaia hypothesis—that the world is best seen as a single organism, of which we are just part. Deep-greens believe that the primary bearer of value is the whole earth, not the individual species on it. The wide-scale human alteration of nature is, on this view, rather like the hand taking over the whole body, so that it is no longer a hand serving the body but the body serving the hand. Likewise, we must serve the earth, not try to make the earth serve us.

I personally find this idea utterly baffling. I cannot see any good reason to suppose that this planet we live on is in any important way like a conscious entity with a point of view. The idea that the world should be seen as a single organism may be a helpful metaphor and it may enable us to consider the interconnectedness of life better. But I cannot see why we should take this metaphor to imply anything else, especially consciousness. The position at least has the merit of some consistency. It provides some coherent rationale for being against large-scale meddling by humans in nature, which less extreme positions cannot. From my point of view, though, the need to accept this rationale is a *reductio ad absurdam* of the whole deep-green ethos. It shows that, taken to its logical conclusion, being against human intervention in nature requires you to value inanimate planets over living, thinking, feeling beings. This is an escape route from the direction my argument is following, but not one I would advise taking.

So, assuming that the environment does not have a point of view and that things cannot go better or worse for it, where does this leave the idea that the environment can be harmed or helped? It certainly does not destroy it. Consider a vase, for example. I do not think that a vase has a point of view, but I do think it can damaged, by being dropped, for example. But—and this is the key point—what determines whether that harm is a good or a bad thing depends not on the vase but upon something with a subjective point of view, a human being. I remember my old school fêtes, where one game was to try to smash old crockery standing on shelf by throwing balls at it. In this context, causing damage to a vase is a positively good thing; it is the whole aim of the activity. So, in one context we can value a vase and want it not to be damaged, and in that instance any harm caused is bad. But in another, we do not value that vase, we want it to be damaged, and in that instance any damage caused is good. In both cases, the good or bad of the harm is determined by the human with a subjective point of view, not the inert vase. If there remains any doubt that harm can be good, just consider how good it is when we harm viruses that threaten our health.

To put this into the language of contemporary philosophy, what we should then say is that the *primary bearers of value* are beings with a point of view. All values have to be traced back to them. Other, inert objects only have value *derivatively*. Vases, for example, derive their value from their usefulness or desirability for humans. In themselves, they have no value. So when we talk about something being harmed or damaged, we can only judge whether this harm or damage is good or bad by reference to primary bearers of value—beings with a point of view. (Alternatively, we could say that a vase, for example, is only really damaged when it undergoes a change we judge to be bad. On this account, I do not damage a vase we want to smash when I smash it. I prefer to stick to the version where we can judge harm to be good, because I think it does justice to the intuitive idea that we can harm something yet judge that was the right thing to do.)

Even this is not the end of the story. Although, on this account, the environment only has derivative value, that does not mean we should not care about it. First, humans are not the only creatures with a point of view. If harming the environment causes things to get worse for other creatures with points of view, that may be a reason to say that harm is bad. But also, if helping the environment causes things to get worse for creatures with a point of view, that is a reason not to help it.

This may sound bizarre so it needs a little explaining. So far, I have avoided the issue of what actually constitutes harm to the environment. I don't think we can actually specify this without making judgements. There does not seem to be any fact of the matter here. For the sake of argument, let us accept the intuitively plausible view that the environment is harmed when there is a decrease in the amount or diversity of life upon it.

Now consider this thought experiment. We discover an airborne virus that will, if left unchecked, wipe out all primates, including humans. We also discover a way of treating this. We can release into the atmosphere something that will kill this virus. But this will also kill a number of plants and animals, resulting in a substantially greater loss of biodiversity than will occur if only primates are wiped out. What should we do?

I hope the answer is obvious. Here, the best thing for the environment is something which wipes out the creatures with the most highly developed subjective points of view, including ourselves. The worst thing for the environment is that which saves us. The thought experiment makes stark the choice we have to face between considering creatures with points of view as the only primary bearers of value and the deep-green view that the environment is of primary value. If we accept that it is right in this instance to save the primates, then one is accepting that harming the environment is not always a bad thing and that we can only determine if it is a bad thing by reference to the interests of creatures with points of view. The alternative is to bite the deep-green bullet and say that the interests of the environment come above those of sentient life. Like many, I would be unable to understand what could motivate that move, other than a false belief that the earth itself is a sentient being worth more than the lives of all the creatures that live upon it.

The view I prefer may not require us to value the environment only to the extent to which it is useful to us. A comparison with the philosophy of art can show why. Some aestheticians argue that a work of art has value only because of what it can mean to creatures capable of aesthetic appreciation. Nevertheless, if one judges something to be a great work of art, one may reasonably want it to be preserved even if it cannot be seen by anyone. The work of art derives its value from the aesthetic appreciation it affords beings like ourselves, but that value resides in the artwork even if it cannot actually be appreciated by anyone. Similarly, we might accept that there is no value in the world without sentient life to value it. But, nevertheless, we can value the environment and want it to be preserved regardless of whether its preservation helps us or not. This desire only becomes morally problematic when we put the interests of the environment above those of the creatures that value it.

Returning to the debate at hand, GM foods are supposed to harm the environment, or at least threaten harm, because their introduction to the environment might lead to a decrease in biodiversity. But even if we accept that this is a harm, and even if we feel that this harm is to be regretted because we value the environment, that is not enough for us to say that this harm is bad. The harm is bad only if it creates a situation which makes life worse for creatures with a point of view, now or in the future. (I have not argued for the view that the interests of creatures with a more developed subjectivity, such as humans and primates, weigh more heavily than those of, say, geese and flies, but I would hope and expect that most would agree with this. The discussions of Chapter 9 are also relevant here.) But if the harm makes things better, then we should allow it.

As can be expected, to judge the likely benefits or costs of GM food to human life requires a clear understanding of the facts. Those who support GM foods often claim that they will allow people in the developing world to grow hardier and healthier crops, thus reducing world hunger. Critics of GM food claim that this is humbug: food supply is not a problem and the multinational manufacturers of GM foods, such as Monsanto, will not use their products to help people but to make profits. (The possibility that one could do both at the same time isn't always considered here.) Once again, this is the point at which the philosopher must retire. The evidence needs to be assessed and other expert views, such as those of economists, NGOs, and scientists carry more weight than those of philosophers.

Of course, part of the debate over GM food is the threat to human health. I have avoided this because, again, this is a matter to be settled by consideration of the evidence. We don't need philosophy to tell us that we do not want to engage on a course of action which will harm humans. Where the philosopher can help is with separating out from this purely pragmatic question other issues which get tangled up in it, such as whether it is right to harm the environment, tamper with nature, or do what is unnatural.

Conclusion

The GM foods debate is difficult, partly because it is very hard to find information which one can trust. The information put out by producers is obviously biased in favour of GM foods, the information put out by environmental groups obviously biased against. When even academic research is often funded by business, it is not always possible to trust its impartiality. For these reasons alone, making judgements about what we read about in the newspapers is a difficult task, though what I said in Chapter 1 should help with this.

The difficulty is not helped by the background in which

broader environmental issues are discussed. The debate is conducted in a vocabulary which is often value-laden, making reasoned judgement more difficult. Philosophy can sensitize us to this and help us see beyond it. There are also certain principles which are implicitly, if not explicitly, accepted, such as the idea that it is wrong to harm the environment or that there is some direct connection between the natural and the good. Philosophy can help us to draw out these implicit principles, analyse them, and see what is and what is not true about them. Philosophy's role here, as elsewhere, is thus less than decisive but more than just incidental.

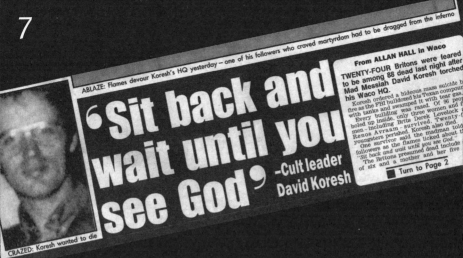

7

ABLAZE: Flames devour Koresh's HQ yesterday — one of his followers who craved martyrdom had to be dragged from the inferno

'Sit back and wait until you see God' —Cult leader David Koresh

CRAZED: Koresh wanted to die

From ALLAN HALL in Waco

TWENTY-FOUR Britons were feared to be among 88 dead last night after Mad Messiah David Koresh torched his Waco HQ.

Koresh ordered a hideous mass suicide b fire as the FBI bulldozed his Texan compoun with tanks and swamped it with tear gas.

Every building was razed. Of 96 peo holed up inside, only three women and f men — including Brits Derek Lovelock a Renos Avraam — survived. Twenty-f youngsters perished. Koresh also died

One survivor said the madman told followers as the flames licked about th "Sit back and wait until you see God."

The Britons presumed dead include of six and a mother and her five

■ Turn to Page 2

Cult friction: Faith and reason

Death in Texas

On 19 April 1993 a fifty-one-day siege near Waco, Texas ended in the deaths of more than eighty people at the compound of the Branch Davidian 'cult' led by David Koresh. From outside the USA, the significance of this event can appear rather small. Here was a loony cult, led by someone with a Messiah complex who, in the end, preferred to burn to death with his followers rather than give in to the authorities. The loss of life was terrible, but it was no more than one in a series of occasional tragedies caused by the misguided beliefs of cults and their members.

But inside the USA, the siege at Waco is seen as much more important than that. For a great many people, this is not just a story about a strange cult. It is a story about religious freedom and the misuse of power by the federal government. From the moment the fire started, many people did not believe that the blaze was a straightforward act of suicide and homicide by Koresh. Many thought the fire was caused by the FBI. In the official version of events, the FBI, constantly communicating with the cult members through megaphones and loudspeakers, fired tear gas into the compound to force them to leave it. Realizing the game was up, it was Koresh or his associates who set the compound ablaze. But many reject this account, saying that the FBI caused the fire, intentionally or through incompetence.

Waco has haunted America ever since. Two years to the day after the Waco blaze, more than 160 people died in the bombing at the Alfred P. Murrah Federal Building in Oklahoma. The man who planted the bomb, Timothy McVeigh, was at least in part motivated to act against the federal government in revenge for what he saw as its culpability for the deaths of the Branch Davidians.

In November 2000, seven years after the tragedy, John Danforth, from the Office of the Special Counsel, finally published his official report into Waco. The report, which ran to several hundred pages and considered an enormous amount of evidence, cleared the federal government and its agents of any wrongdoing, placing the blame for the fire squarely at the feet of Koresh. But that was not the end of the matter. Many rejected the findings of the report. The libertarian Cato Institute, for example, published a report the following year, describing the Danforth investigation as 'soft and incomplete', complaining that many crimes on the federal side had gone unpunished. The Cato Institute is not an extreme religious organization. Its board of directors is comprised mainly of senior business people, including David Koch, Executive Vice President of Koch Industries, and Rupert Murdoch, Chairman and CEO of the News Corporation. The Internet is awash with sites critical of the federal government and sympathetic to the Davidians.

Behind this story lie many issues, many of which are specifically about the relationship between the American people and its federal government. The questions of what actually happened at the siege and who is to blame are not ones I attempt to answer here (although what I say in Chapter 1 is relevant to how we judge which account is correct). More philosophically interesting is what Waco shows about where we draw the line between legitimate religious belief and cult quackery. My guess is that, in Europe, the vast majority would say that the Branch Davidians had crossed that line. In the United States, however, many more people would see the Branch Davidians as belonging to the family of legitimate religious movements.

This question of where to draw this line comes up quite regularly in the news. In recent years, there has been a long-running controversy over the German government's refusal to recognize the Church of Scientology as a bona fide religious movement. In China, the Fulan Gong movement has been persecuted by the authorities. The harsh nature of this persecution means that most in the West are against it. But the question of whether China is right to want to contain the movement or whether it is both legitimate and harmless still demands an answer.

Untangling these issues requires us to look at philosophical issues concerning the foundation and justification of religious belief. To begin with, I will look at whether a simple distinction can be made between a cult and a religion, before going on to consider the implications of this discussion for how we understand the relationship between faith and reason more generally.

What is a cult?

The distinction between a religion and cult might be thought to be a very important one. In general, people are opposed to cults and consider them sinister or threatening, whereas religions are seen as benign and are often given more respect than other belief systems. However, the distinction is extremely problematic and in recent years non-mainstream religions have gone to great lengths to avoid being stigmatized as cults.

The most interesting example of this is the story of the Cult Awareness Network (CAN), an anti-cult organization which collected and disseminated information about cults. Not surprisingly, many non-mainstream religions objected to being categorized by CAN as cults, and there is indeed a serious issue here about who has the authority to assign this negative label to a religion. CAN found itself at the receiving end of several lawsuits and as a result of losing one was declared bankrupt in 1996. The same year, the CAN logos and trademarks were sold in a federal bankruptcy court to a law firm associated with one of the religions CAN had criticized, the Church of Scientology. The new CAN now presents 'information' in defence of many of the organizations that the old CAN denounced as cults. According to the new CAN website, 'Over the past two decades alone, the word "cult" has been transformed into a by-word used to slanderously label legitimate religious groups as inauthentic and even harmful, creating a climate in which individual adherents are being deprived of their inalienable rights to practice their religion freely, as their conscience directs.' CAN prefers the *Oxford English Dictionary* definition of a cult as ' . . . a particular form or system of religious belief . . . '.

In this climate, it is clear that nothing uncontroversial can be said about what precisely constitutes a cult. Even the old CAN did not attempt a simple definition, but instead listed what it saw as the distinctive marks of a *destructive* cult. These were: mind control, charismatic leadership, deception, exclusivity, alienation, exploitation, and a totalitarian world-view (we/they syndrome). This is broadly what most people would accept as the characteristic features of a cult.

Philosophy, especially in the Western Anglo-American tradition, is fond of making conceptual distinctions. For that reason it might seem that philosophy can be of some assistance here. The trouble is that the history of philosophy is as much about showing why certain conceptual distinctions are problematic as it is about making clear, uncontroversial ones. Nevertheless, there is a general lesson we can learn about philosophy concerning distinctions such as those between a religion and a cult. This point can be illustrated by the famous Sorites paradox, attributed to the Greek philosopher Eubulides, who lived in the fourth century BC.

In one version of this paradox we have to imagine someone who is without any doubt tall, say 2.5 metres. Consider now whether that person would still be tall if they were 0.1 mm shorter. The answer surely has to be that they would still be tall. The reason for this is simple: 0.1 mm is an insignificant distance with regard to the height of persons. So it seems that if anyone is tall, then a person 0.1 mm shorter than this would still be tall.

The problem is that if 'tall person − 0.1 mm = tall person', then someone 0.1 mm shorter again than this tall person would also be tall. But if we carried on like this—always accepting that a person 0.1 mm shorter than someone we accept is tall is themselves tall—eventually we'd end up with someone who was, say, one metre tall and we'd have to say that they too were tall. And that would just be absurd.

One moral of this story might be that you can have two quite different concepts—in this instance, tall and short—and yet not be able to specify any strict rule which tells you when each should be applied. In this instance, it just seems absurd to suggest that there is some height, 0.1 mm above which a person should be considered tall and from that height down be considered short, or average height. (Some philosophers, however, have accepted this apparent absurdity.) The truth revealed by the paradox could thus be that it is possible both that there is a real and important difference between two concepts and yet at the same time it is impossible to draw a sharp dividing line to show where each applies. A clearly tall person is very different physically from a clearly short one, even though there are other people for whom it is not clear whether they should be called tall or short.

If we apply this insight to cults and religions, we can see that it may be impossible to state with any precision a sharp difference between religions and cults. Nevertheless, that is not to say the difference between them isn't real and important. This point is reinforced if we look again at the old CAN's list of the hallmarks of a destructive cult. Many of these hallmarks are also borne by mainstream religions. There are many charismatic leaders in mainstream Christianity, Judaism, and Islam, not least Christ, Abraham, and Mohamed. All of these religions can be accused of exclusivity and alienation. Christ, for example, reputedly said, 'If anyone is coming to Me and is not hating his father and mother and wife and children and brothers and sisters, and still more his soul besides, he can not be My disciple' (Luke 14: 26). This insistence that followers turn against their families is precisely what many cults are accused of doing. It is hard to imagine a more exclusive doctrine than the Jewish idea that they are God's chosen people. The totalitarian world-view or 'we/they' syndrome is also often present in mainstream religion, with the distinction between believers and infidels, the saved and the damned. 'He who is not with Me is against Me', Christ is reported to have said (John 11: 23).

We could go even further. It could be argued that mainstream religions practise mind control. Most religions tend to encourage the repetition of sacred texts or prayers, chanting or singing, devotion to reading religious writings to the exclusion of anything which might challenge or go against it. The fact that such techniques are quite subtle and are not obviously coercive may even be a reason to argue that they are more dangerous: the most effective mind control is that which does not appear to be mind control at all.

Even on the counts of deception and exploitation mainstream religions do not come off unscathed. There have been many instances of both in the history of religion. For example, such was the volume of complaints about sexual abuse by Roman Catholic clergy worldwide that in November 2001 the Pope issued a general apology to all the nuns and others who had been its victims. He also acknowledged that the Church had failed to eradicate these abuses. One cannot help feeling that a similar acknowledgement by a cult leader would not have been received so sanguinely.

It should also be remembered that not all so-called cults have all these features anyway. Not all are deceptive, for example. Many are run by sincere people who genuinely believe what they teach. Some can only be consistently accused of using mind control techniques if mainstream religions are too.

So the line between religions and cults certainly is blurred, as is the line between tall and short. That doesn't mean that some organizations cannot be clearly identified as destructive cults, just as some people clearly are tall. If an organization displays all the characteristics on old CAN's checklist, then we can say with certainty it is a cult. If a religion eschews mind control, exploitation, and deception, then even if it has some of the other features of a cult, it does not merit the label. We must not make the mistake of thinking that because the area in the middle is blurred, there is no difference at either end.

One difference between this kind of blurred boundary and that between the tall and the short is that there is a value-laden dimension to the judgement as to whether or not a movement is a cult or not. In philosophical jargon, we might say that there is a *normative* element in the identification of a religion as a cult. Whether or not the Branch Davidians, for example, constitute a cult is not a simple matter of fact. To say it is or is not a cult is to make an evaluation which not only goes beyond the mere facts but also brings with it a value judgement. In other words, the decision is not fully *rationally determined* by the facts. But as long as we think that the term 'cult' has some meaningful application, the evaluation cannot be avoided, because we are making a judgement whether we decide a movement is not a cult just as much as if we decide it is. Even when we say we cannot decide whether a movement is a cult, we are making a judgement that it occupies the grey area between cult and religion.

To say such normative judgements are not rationally *determined* is not to say they are not rationally *constrained*. Our judgements are constrained by rationality to the extent that we cannot just label any movement a cult by pure whim. There need to be reasons for calling something a cult, reasons which are provided by rational considerations of what a cult is and about the particular movement in question. These reasons are not sufficient to settle the matter beyond dispute—hence the judgement is not rationally determined—but they do place limits on the range of judgements that can reasonably be made—hence the judgement is rationally constrained.

This is an important point, because people sometimes make the mistake of thinking that when reason cannot settle a question conclusively, rational considerations become irrelevant. This misrepresents the role of rationality in our lives. Most of our rational decision-making is not about finding rationally conclusive arguments for believing or doing something. Rather, it is about making a decision which is not rationally determined but which is rationally informed. As John Searle has put it, there is always a gap between the reasons we have for performing an action and the decision actually to act, a gap he argues is filled by the exercise of free choice. For example, if I decide which car to buy, it is not usually the case that, if I sit down and think about it rationally, I will see that one car must be the best choice. But nor is it the case that rational reflection has no role to play in my decision. What actually tends to happen is that I sit down and think about the pros and cons of various cars and having become rationally informed, I make a personal decision. Someone else, with the same information and no more or less rational than me, might chose a different car. Both our choices, though different, are more rational than the choice of the person who just goes out and buys the first car she sees.

Is the Branch Davidian faith a cult?

In saying that the Branch Davidian faith is a cult (or not), we are then making a rationally informed judgement, not just describing a simple fact. The question now arises, why would we want to make such a judgement? The reason is simple: in the phrase of the old CAN, there do exist 'destructive cults'. If there were nothing harmful in cults, then whether or not we described a movement as a cult would be a kind of intellectual game of no importance. But since we believe genuine cults are harmful, the decision as to whether a movement merits the label 'cult' is hardly trivial.

So whether we say the Branch Davidians form a cult or not depends on whether we think they have enough of the harmful characteristics of a cult, like those described by the old CAN. Anyone who accepts the Danforth report would have to accept that the Davidians are a cult in this sense. The history of the movement, an offshoot of the Seventh Day Adventist Church, is a story of internecine power struggles between factions loyal to individual charismatic leaders. Koresh taught that God deceives people and that he was permitted to deceive others to ensure their salvation, thus officially enshrining deception in the religion itself. The movement was certainly exclusive, in that the Davidians believed that they would be at the centre of the great war at the end of time and would be saved by God. As for exploitation, Koresh took several 'wives', including a 12- and a 14-year-old girl as his second and third wives, both in 1986.

Of course, if we agree that the Branch Davidians are a cult, we still have to decide what to do about them. One could agree that it is a cult and still fiercely disagree with the actions of the federal forces at Waco. One could argue that cults should be outlawed, that there should be freely available information on them or that there should be a 'free market' in religious belief and people should be able to join cults if they want. Neither the recognition of what a cult is nor the judgement that certain movements are genuine cults automatically generates a policy decision. That requires more, perhaps even harder, thinking.

News as a mirror

Most of this book is concerned with how one can use philosophy to understand better the issues behind current affairs. However, I do not think that there should only be one-way traffic here, with oneself using philosophy to illuminate the news. The news, thus illuminated, can cast light on our own beliefs and encourage further reflection on them.

This is particularly evident in the case of Waco because of what the story reveals about the relationship between mainstream religion and cults. The nature of this distinction should cause concern to serious religious believers for several reasons.

First, the fact that the line between the two is blurred should prompt a serious examination of one's own creeds. If, in essence, the difference is essentially about harm, one must ask if one's own religion is harmful. Many atheists would argue that at least some denominations of mainstream religions are harmful. Let us set aside fundamentalist Islam for the moment as enough has already been said by others about its dangers. We can find plenty of other examples from the Judeo-Christian tradition. For instance, there are people who grow up seriously scarred by a particularly harsh form of Catholic upbringing. Feelings of guilt and self-loathing can be inculcated by this kind of religious background. Of course, I am not suggesting that Catholicism is necessarily harmful in the way that many cults are, but the fact that it can cause harm should make adherents of the faith sit up and take notice. It would be hypocritical to tut-tut the harms of cults when similar harms, albeit it on a lesser scale, are being caused within one's own faith. If it's wrong when a cult does it, it's wrong when a mainstream religion does it.

Evangelical Christianity also has its dangers. In Britain in 1999, a young girl, Victoria Climbié, died after having suffered long-term abuse and neglect by her aunt, who was her guardian, in Haringey, London. The aunt was a member of the evangelical Universal Church of the Kingdom of God and took her there to be exorcized, a service the church often provides. Pastor Alvaro Lima from that church saw Victoria twice in the week before her death and failed to report his concerns to social services. Could he really have doubted for one minute that abuse rather than Satanic possession was the cause of her dreadful physical condition? It is hard to read about this terrible story without feeling that this church distorts the minds of its members and inculcates in them beliefs which are not only harmful, but in this case may have stopped someone preventing the death of a young girl.

The second cause of concern for mainstream religious believers is that we usually think it is not just the fact that a religion is harmful that makes it a cult. Rather, we tend to dismiss the beliefs of cults as 'wacky' or insane. In fact, it would be very hard to distinguish between mainstream religion and cults on this basis. It is surely only our familiarity with or acceptance of Christianity which prevents us from seeing its ritual consumption of 'blood and flesh', its belief in the virgin birth, and its central Messiah figure of God made man as bizarre. Koresh believed the Davidians were a chosen people who would be led back to Palestine for the end of the world. Similar beliefs are Jewish orthodoxy.

What our considerations about Waco have done is to shine a light on the problematic relationship between faith and reason. The fact is that cults can only be consistently defined and opposed on grounds of their harmfulness. If we tried to make irrationality a criterion for a religion being a cult, then mainstream religions would find themselves in the dock as well. This is an important issue so I want to spend some time looking at it a little closer.

Faith and reason

The problem for mainstream religion is that it relies upon the idea that a lot of its creeds are essentially mysterious—they fall beyond the scope of rationality. That is not to say it is irrational to believe in God, merely that belief in God is not fully subject to rational scrutiny. Reason can only take us so far with religion: beyond that lie mysteries, which to believe we must rely on faith.

This idea of reason having its limits can be broken down into three distinct components. We can say that there is a limit to what we can *understand* in respect to religion; we can say there is a limit to what we can *know* about God; and we can say that there is a limit to how far we can *justify* religious belief by reason. Here I want to focus on the third of these, as this is most directly relevant to the division between cults and religions. What we are talking about here is faith. The idea is that though certain beliefs can be justified by reason, some beliefs cannot. Beliefs that are not justified by reason are justified by faith. Faith is therefore defined as the holding of a belief which cannot be rationally justified. That is why the inability to provide rational arguments for the existence of God is actually sometimes held to be a good thing, for if one could prove that God existed, there would be no need for faith. As faith is essential to religious belief, it seems a good thing that we lack the proof for God's existence, which would make faith unnecessary.

We may wonder why it is that faith has been elevated to such a high position in religion. Christianity in particular has praised those whose belief is founded on faith, rather than proof, as the story of 'doubting Thomas' shows. But if one steps outside religion for a moment, it is hard to see why faith should be considered superior to justified belief. If I try to sell you a new remedy for headaches, it would be odd to say that you are a better person if you accept my remedy on faith than if you demanded to know the evidence for its efficacy. We also know that 'trust me' is the plea most often uttered by those who know that they should never be trusted at all. And while in common speech it is perhaps admirable to 'have faith' in someone who has proved themselves reliable in the past, it is just foolish to do so with strangers or those who have proved themselves to be unreliable.

However, my main concern here is not with the value of faith, but rather that the full implications of taking one's beliefs on faith are properly understood. Faith is often seen as reassuring and comforting. Yet the most insightful analysis of faith I have come across is *Fear and Trembling* by the Danish existentialist, Søren Kierkegaard. Why 'fear and trembling'? Kierkegaard asks us to consider the case of Abraham, usually held up as the prime example of the man of faith. He was asked by God to kill his only son and went on to attempt to do so. This might seem a reasonable thing to do. After all, if God tells you to do something, you do it. But imagine you are Abraham. Was that God telling you to do that, or was it a malicious demon, or just voices in your head? Peter Sutcliffe, the 'Yorkshire ripper', between 1975 and 1980 mutilated and killed thirteen women, and attempted to murder a further six because he thought God had told him to do so. Could you be like him? Could it be that you are not being called by God, but you're just sick? That would make more sense. After all, God is loving and kind, and yet he asks you to make a human sacrifice. If you go ahead with the sacrifice you are doing what by all standards of reason and morality is simply nuts. Yet without any rational justification for what you do, you do it anyway, because you have faith. Fear and trembling? You'd better believe it.

Abraham's case is particularly difficult, but let's take ordinary belief in God. If your belief is genuinely based on faith, then it is, by definition, belief without rational justification. Many beliefs lack rational justification. There is the belief that one will not die if one jumps off a thirty-storey building. There is the belief that all politicians are puppets of mind-controlling aliens. There is also the belief that the universe is shaped like a banana. To this group, we can add religious beliefs. If one tries to distinguish these beliefs from the others on this list by appealing to reason, one is undermining one's claim that one's belief is a matter of faith. The shocking thing about faith is precisely that it lacks a rational basis and so from an objective, rational point of view, is on a par with the other beliefs in the list. The challenge of faith is precisely to accept this and believe it anyway. To do so, I believe, requires us to stop thinking about faith as a soothing panacea for the failings of reason and to start thinking of it as the terrifying leap characterized by Kierkegaard.

This is why a religious believer cannot distinguish his or her own beliefs from those of most cults simply on the grounds of rationality. For both cults and mainstream religions, Branch Davidians and Roman Catholics, if faith truly is the basis of belief, then the fact that the beliefs are not rationally justified isn't just acceptable, it's essential. But if faith is an acceptable basis of belief for mainstream religious believers, why isn't it an acceptable basis of belief for cult members? The believer is thus faced with a two-pronged dilemma. Following one prong, one can accept that faith is an acceptable basis for belief, but that requires us to grant the same respect to cult beliefs as to mainstream religions, unless one is more or less harmful than the other. The other prong is to reject the idea that faith is a legitimate basis for belief and that requires us to grant the same disrespect to mainstream religions as we do to cults.

Intuition and feeling

It could be argued that I have missed the point in making a stark contrast between faith and reason. Faith may not be grounded in reason, but that does not mean it is grounded in nothing at all. Faith can be grounded in intuition or feeling. The religious do not believe because of rational arguments but rather because they have a feeling or intuition of God's presence. Why not accept the role feeling and intuition have to play in our awareness of the divine? Why privilege reason?

There are two reasons why we should be very wary of trusting our feelings when it comes to belief about the world around and even beyond us. First of all, our intuitions are terribly unreliable. Sure, many of us are pretty good at sensing what other people are thinking, feeling, or about to do. But when it comes to our ideas about the external world, our intuitions are often horribly wrong. For example, intuition says that a heavy object falls faster than a light one, but it doesn't. Intuition says that objects will fly off a spinning sphere, not get pulled towards it, yet gravity pulls us towards the spinning earth all the time. Intuition says that time ticks away at the same speed wherever you are, yet the astronaut who returns to earth has lived fewer minutes than his counterpart who stays put. Put simply, when it comes to knowledge about the external world, and even more when it comes to knowledge of the fundamental nature of reality, intuition is a hopeless guide. Why then trust it when it tells you there is a God?

Secondly, intuitions and feelings conflict when it comes to God. People do have very profound religious experiences, the world over, and these persuade people, not on the basis of argument, but on feeling, that such and such a religious being exists. And yet what for one person confirms in their mind the existence of Jesus Christ, persuades someone else equally that Vishnu exists. Of course, it is the very nature of such experiences that they exert a powerful grip. But as soon as we recognize that others have similar experiences which persuade them of quite the contrary, we are faced with a difficulty. We could say that our experience reveals a truth which the others' experiences do not. But then that seems to be an extremely arrogant view to take. It is to believe that our conviction of the meaning of our experience is somehow more valid than someone else's conviction about their experiences, even though to an impartial observer both experiences would appear equally impressive. Much more reasonable would be to accept that such experiences, since they lead people to believe different and conflicting things, are just not a good ground for belief at all. They are simply unreliable guides.

Consider the following analogy. If I telephone the train timetables enquiry line and get a different, conflicting answer as to what time my train goes every time, I would conclude that it was an unreliable source of knowledge about train times. If I consult people's feelings about whether God exists or not, and if so, which God he is, and I get many different answers, I should conclude that people's feelings are an unreliable guide to God's existence. Having reached that conclusion, it would be unreasonable of me to make my own feelings an exception to the rule. We are all prone to feeling that everyone else's intuitions are unreliable except our own, but I hope we all have the self-awareness to accept that, on reflection, such a conviction is nothing more than self-delusion and arrogance.

One objection that is increasingly raised these days is that it may be true that everyone's religious beliefs could be essentially right, that we each know God through our own faiths and so though it is true people disagree about God, that doesn't matter.

Much could be said about this (see the discussion on crude rela-tivism in Chapter 1), but I think that this sweet pill has at least one more unpalatable consequence. In order for it be true that, for example, a Christian and a Hindu could both be right, then either we have to give up the idea that there is objective truth—which seems counter to the spirit of a religious conception that, after all, asserts that God is the absolute truth—or we have to dilute the specific features of each religion to such an extent that they lose what makes them distinctive, clear beliefs at all. For example, how can it be true that there is only one God (Christi-anity) and many gods (Hinduism)? Only if the sense in which there is one or many gods is so loose that it is hard to see what sense there is in asserting either. So to accept the equal validity of all religions requires one to give up many of the beliefs that characterize one's faith in the first place.

Of course, the other problem with accepting intuition and feeling as a basis for belief is that we are faced with the same two-pronged dilemma as was faced by the acceptance of faith. Following one prong, one can accept that intuition is an acceptable basis for faith, but that requires us to grant the same respect to cult beliefs as to mainstream religions. The other prong is to reject the idea that intuition is a legitimate basis for faith and that requires us to grant the same dis-respect to mainstream religions as we do to cults. This emphasizes the broader point about irrationality, religion, and cults. Instinctively people tend to feel that cult beliefs are less rational than those of established religions. But, in fact, both cults and mainstream religions depend upon limiting the role of rationality to such an extent that rationality becomes virtually irrelevant. The consequences of this for religious believers are serious indeed.

Conclusion

The Waco tragedy is an interesting example of a news story that is interpreted very differently depending on where the reporting is made. If we ask whether the Branch Davidians are a cult or a respectable religion, our starting assumptions may be very different if we're an average Briton or an average American. It is important to remember this in order to get to the truth in the news we read and hear. Sometimes, we may appear to get a diversity of opinion across our media, but we may find that the range of opinion offered is different from what we would find in foreign media. With the internet it is now possible to see how international stories are reported abroad. Perhaps we should make more of an effort to do so.

Whatever your starting assumptions, on examination the Waco story does reveal how hard it is to make a clear and fair distinction between religions and cults. What we need to do is perhaps worry less about what label the news media places on a religious group and see for ourselves whether it is harmful or benign. This, at the end of the day, is a more important question than whether it is a religion or a cult.

That is obviously not the end of the discussion. What I have outlined here is a challenge to the religious believer who believes their own beliefs are very different from those of cult members such as the Branch Davidians. One cannot think about an event such as the inferno at Waco in a vacuum. The philosophy one applies and the conclusions one comes to have implications for our own beliefs. This is what I meant earlier when I said that, if we illuminate our understanding of current affairs with philosophy, those same events will in turn cast light on our own beliefs. A serious philosophical engagement with the news of the day is thus a two-way process.

8

Bread and circuses: Calculating value

Costs and benefits

To celebrate the new millennium, a temporary exhibition was held in London throughout the whole of the year 2000. This exhibition was housed in a huge futuristic dome, built on disused, contaminated land, which was cleaned up prior to its construction. New transport infrastructure and housing were also part of this regeneration project. The exhibition consisted of several 'zones' where families could explore themes such as the body, faith, and discovery. There was also a spectacular show in the Dome's central arena.

Six and a half million people visited the exhibition during the course of the year, more than double the number who visited Britain's second most popular attraction. This made the Dome the second most popular visitor attraction in Europe. Independent surveys showed around nine out of ten visitors were satisfied with their visit.

So was the millennium Dome a success? According the media, it was not. It seemed that almost every day, from months before the Dome's opening to months after it finally closed, there would be a negative media story about it somewhere. Many thought the exhibition vacuous and facile, a dumbed-down theme park of little worth. The project also suffered because, for reasons which have never been clear, the original business plan forecast twelve million visitors, a figure most agree was ludicrously high. The repeated failure to meet these unrealistic targets made the Dome seem more of a failure than it actually was.

But the single largest complaint about the Dome was its excessive cost. Over £600 million was spent on the Dome—

nearly $1,000 million. This money did not come directly from the taxpayer's pocket, but from the Millennium Commission, which was responsible for distributing money raised by the British national lottery. This money is part of the lottery revenue reserved for 'good causes', which include arts and culture. For many, this was an unacceptable waste of money. Think of the good use this money could have been put to in health care or education. To spend it instead on a middle-brow theme park, which people still had to spend money to get into, seems wrong.

On other occasions, however, there are no complaints when money which could have been spent on health and education goes instead to less urgent causes. The year 2000 also saw the opening of the Tate Modern museum, housed in a converted power station on London's Bankside. Media commentators could not resist comparing the glories of Tate Modern to the follies of the Dome at every conceivable opportunity. At a cost of £134 million to build and more than £25 million of public money every year to run and maintain free entry, the gallery was judged to be a bargain by most, especially in comparison to the Dome.

For most people, just thinking about the sums of money involved in such projects is dizzying. It can seem hard to justify spending such huge sums of money on arts and leisure (or even the US space programme) when so many basic public services are inadequate. When one considers how far the money spent on such projects would have gone on other more obviously urgent causes, such spending can look like waste. Indeed, the phrase most often used when complaining about state spending like this is that it is 'a waste of taxpayers' money'.

Many have judged the Dome to be waste of taxpayers'

money, even though the money spent on it came almost entirely out of lottery funds rather than from tax revenues. Most in the media have judged that Tate Modern was a good use of tax-payers' money, though it is not clear how many non-museum-going users of the National Health Service would agree if they knew the costs involved. Which, if any, of these judgements are correct? To answer these questions fully requires a consideration of several issues, many of which are not at all philosophical. For example, there is the question of financial management and planning: were the costs of these projects kept as low as possible by those running them? This is a question for accountants, not philosophers. Then there is the question of the quality of these specific projects, rather than of the general value of art and entertainment. Whether we judge the Tate was good value at £134 million obviously depends in part on whether we think the end result is a high-quality gallery. This is a question for critics, commentators, and the public that visits the attractions, not philosophers.

A full answer does, however, require us to address some philosophical issues. One such issue concerns the proper role of the state. We may think, for example, that the Tate Modern is a worthwhile and wonderful gallery, but that it is not the business of the state to build and run such arts centres. Another import-ant philosophical issue, which is the one I wish to look at first, is the question of what gives something value in the first place. This might seem a little esoteric, but it lies at the heart of the debate over the Dome and Tate Modern. Our judgements as to the merits of these projects is informed largely by whether we think they result in something worthwhile and valuable. The

Dome was seen as shallow and frivolous, and thus possessing little value. That is one main reason why there were complaints that so much money was spent on it. Tate Modern, on the other hand, is seen as a world-class gallery and a valuable addition to the nation's heritage. That is one main reason why people are not so worried about how much it cost. The fact that the Tate Modern cost less than the Dome must surely be irrelevant to most people's judgements, since such vast sums as £134 million or £628 million are equally incomprehensible to the person in the street. In short, both are inconceivable amounts of money that could have been used to provide so many hospital beds. But since Tate Modern was liked by media commentators and popular with the public, the number of hospital beds that could have been provided instead is seen as irrelevant.

What this shows, I think, is that we have a very rough and ready grasp of the concept of value and that, when we compare the value of different things, we do so in a very crude way. This is partly because such comparisons are often by their nature vague. For example, I'm not sure that there is any sensible way one could rigorously compare the value of an art gallery and a hospital, for reasons which will become clear. Accountants would talk about cost/benefits analysis, but the problem here is that when the benefits are not just financial, we have to resort again to informed judgement rather than arithmetic. When building a road you can compare the economic benefits it will bring with the cost of construction. To do the same with an art gallery seems to miss the point of what the value of such an institution is.

So what does it mean to say something has value? In the

dialogues of Plato, Socrates often used to try to answer a question like this by proposing (or more usually asking other people to propose) a preliminary definition of the concept he sought to understand. By probing and examining this concept, he aimed to see what truth, if any, was contained in this answer. In a similar way, I want to answer this question by proposing a general form of answer and then scrutinizing it to fill in the detail. The preliminary definition I want to consider is the idea that something has value if it satisfies a need. What I mean by this will become clearer once we examine some of the different needs we as humans have.

Needs and value

A friend of mine once packed up work for a few months and went off travelling in India. While she was away I met someone who asked after her. He wanted to know why she had gone away. I said it was just for the experience of travelling and seeing new places. My acquaintance looked blank and replied, 'No reason, then'.

Because my answer had not revealed any practical need the trip was fulfilling—such as to learn a new language or increase skills—my acquaintance thought there was no reason or value in it. He couldn't see what purpose or use the trip could serve and so he thought it literally pointless.

Engineers build bridges, doctors save lives, farmers provide food, and all of these serve practical needs. The same could be said for hairdressers, traffic wardens, and shelf-stackers. All of these jobs have practical consequences—they help us to go about our lives in a way which is either easier or more pleasant than it would otherwise be. It is very easy to compare theoretical, artistic, or sporting pursuits to these and find them useless in comparison. I remember a Ph.D. student in biochemistry who took the attitude, 'my research might help the search for a cure for cancer—what will yours do?'

This kind of reaction astonishes me since it surely takes a moment's reflection to realize that our needs are for more than the purely 'practical'. For a start, most so-called practical pursuits are no more than means to an end. They don't directly provide the things that make life worthwhile, they merely remove some of life's difficulties so that we can get on with pursuing what is of real value to us. Take engineering as an example. Thanks to engineers, we can build better bridges. What's good about that? Well, a bridge in the right spot can make travel easier. That's a good thing, not because travelling by car is in itself a good thing that we want to encourage (far from it—most car journeys are a burden to those who undertake them and diminish the pleasantness of our environment) but because we need to travel for our work and leisure. In the case of work, that may not in itself be a particularly good thing either. Many work primarily in order to earn the money they need to get the things they want and need from life. And what are those things? They vary, but they may include a good standard of living, loving relationships, friends, and material comfort—the things that make life worth living.

These are the things we really want, not bridges. Bridges merely help us get them. The point may seem obvious, but we often lose sight of it. Even with medicine, the good thing about saving lives is that it enables us to get on with life. Surgery is not a good thing in itself. Quite the opposite: if I could go my whole life without surgery I'd be very relieved. All the practical professions are there merely to serve a greater good—the good of living a satisfying and full life. So before we assert the moral superiority of the practical professions over the rest, we should remember that the practical is in the service of humanity and not the other way around. Practical skills help satisfy our basic needs, they don't necessarily help satisfy all of our deepest needs. Practical skills help us to live our lives, they are not what makes living those lives worthwhile.

One reason for this confusion is that there are two ways in which a need can be judged to be important. This can be made clear by considering the humanist psychologist Abraham Maslow's hierarchy of human needs. At the bottom of this hierarchy are material and physical needs for basic existence. In the middle come needs for relationships, personal and social. At the top come needs for personal growth, including needs for the aesthetic, understanding, and self-actualization. Maslow's theory concerns motivation and is based on the idea that we only seek to satisfy needs higher up the hierarchy once we have satisfied those lower down.

One can disagree with the specifics of Maslow's theory, but there is clear sense in the general idea of the hierarchy of needs. The interest for us is that the hierarchy shows that there are two different ways in which we can identify needs as important. Looked at in one way, the most important needs are those at the bottom of the hierarchy, since unless these are satisfied, we cannot do anything at all. But looked at in another way, the most important needs are at the top of the hierarchy, as these express our highest aspirations as human beings.

How does this impact on the idea that something has value if it satisfies a need? First, it makes it clear that we have a whole range of needs, and that those needs satisfied by what we tend to call the 'practical' lie only at the bottom of the hierarchy. Second, it shows how it is too simplistic to say that our material needs are more important. They are more important in the sense that they alone are indispensable, but it is their absence we feel most acutely, not their presence. We positively value most those things which satisfy our higher needs; we value the things that satisfy our lower needs only to the extent that we need them to carry on living.

Returning to the Dome, Tate Modern, and health, we can now see how hospital beds have value because they meet our most basic needs. Tate Modern has value because it meets our higher need for aesthetic experience. And, despite what its critics say, the Millennium Dome can also be seen to have value because it meets our needs for knowledge and—to a certain extent—for aesthetic experience too. What is more, the Dome was very much a 'family day out' and in providing a focus for such an activity, it helps meet some of our interpersonal needs.

Cynics might scoff at this point, thinking I cannot be serious about the Dome's ability to meet needs for knowledge and aesthetic experience. Well, I have to confess what many of the Dome's critics do not—that I never visited it. But from the endless coverage of the exhibition, it seems that the reason people do not take this claim seriously is that the knowledge imparted at the exhibition was quite insubstantial and as an aesthetic experience it was hardly high art. But the exhibition was aimed mainly at children and ordinary families. It was not designed to meet the needs of the highly educated or art lovers, so it had little value to them. It is short-sighted to say that because something doesn't meet your needs it has no value at all, and downright elitist to say that because the needs being met were not those of the most educated that it is somehow of lesser value.

This is a point worth dwelling on, because we have to remember that the media consists mostly of educated middle-class city-dwellers. In Britain, these people almost all live in and around London. The perception these journalists have of what is of most value and importance is not unrelated to what their own needs are. Perhaps the most striking example of this is the media obsession in Britain with the state of the railways. The fact of the matter is that most working-class people rarely take the train. When using public transport, they use the bus far more. Trains are used most heavily by middle-class commuters and business travellers. Buses are often slow, irregular, and crowded. Yet there is no media clamour to improve our bus services. There are probably several reasons for this, but one is almost certainly the fact that journalists see most value in what they need, and they need a better train service more than they need better buses.

Bread and circuses

The idea that all sorts of things, not only essential, practical services, have value because they satisfy a wide range of human needs should not be too controversial. However, this still leaves the other philosophical question I raised unanswered: what role should the state play in satisfying these needs? The fact that the Dome satisfies some need does not in itself justify the state spending £628 million pounds on it. Professional football matches have value because they satisfy some human needs— often more for the interpersonal needs for belonging than for entertainment. But we do not in general think that the state should go around subsidizing football matches. This reflects the general idea that it is not the state's role to satisfy all our human needs. Indeed, in the liberal West, we find the very idea of a state which tries to do this oppressive. The general liberal view is that the state should satisfy only those needs which it is best equipped to satisfy, and should as much as possible leave us free as individuals to satisfy our other needs according to our choices. This is partly because we value our ability to 'self-actualize', to cultivate our own personal growth, and this requires an independence which is undermined by a patrician state which tries to determine what all our needs are and then meet them.

On the other hand, states have never concerned themselves purely with practical services and infrastructure. The old Roman idea that the state should provide 'bread and circuses' has been extremely resilient. On this view, the state needs to provide some public spectacles in addition to making sure people's basic needs are met. At the heart of this idea is the insight, surely correct, that a happy, healthy, content society needs more than just essential services. It needs a civic life, entertainment, and culture.

The idea, however, that the state should do more than provide basic services but less than try to satisfy all the needs we have is not very helpful in practice. Two major questions still remain. The first concerns how much the state should provide beyond basic services. The answer one gives to this question will depend very much on the broader view one takes of the state's role. Advocates of the minimal state will obviously oppose government spending on anything which is not either essential or can be done much more efficiently than in the private sector. There are also deep-rooted cultural differences which cannot be ignored. In Spain, for example, there are a lot of free festivities and cultural activities paid for from the public purse, many more than in Britain, where both national and local government are much more frugal in their spending on such things. In North America, more money is spent by individuals on health care than by the state, in contrast to Europe where typically 70–80 per cent of total spending on health is by the government. These differences in part reflect different attitudes to public and civic life, which must be taken into account when coming up with any prescriptions.

The other reason the question 'how much?' is hard to answer is because it depends on what other needs and priorities are urgent at the time. What would be an acceptable outlay for a prosperous nation in good economic times might be sheer folly to a struggling developing nation, or a developed one during a recession.

The other question concerns the type of activity which the state should support. It is interesting to note that, while the Romans provided circuses—popular entertainment for the masses—modern Western nations tend to subsidize high art. As has been noted, art galleries rather than football clubs benefit from state support. When the state did try to subsidize a 'circus'—the Millennium Dome—the result was outcry, criticism, and ridicule.

The great Russian writer Leo Tolstoy, in his *What is Art?* produced a provocative argument against the public subsidy of the arts. Tolstoy thought that art is based on the 'capacity of man to receive another man's expression of feeling and experience those feelings himself'. The quality of a work of art is then partially determined by the success of this transmission of feeling. However, in order properly to assess the value of a work of art we need to decide whether the feelings (and thoughts) being transmitted are worthy ones. Only this can provide an objective measure of a work of art's value. All other judgements are by their nature subjective. An opera that moves one person to tears can bore another to death (and frequently does).

There are obvious problems with Tolstoy's theory. Most strikingly, it has the consequence that it renders his own masterpieces worthless while elevating the status of his lesser, didactic short stories. Another problem is that the objective measure of value Tolstoy seeks is only there if we accept an objective moral system, such as the Christian ethics Tolstoy followed. However, if one accepts the general point that there can be no objective assessment of the value of the kind of aesthetic pleasure a work of art gives, then this has consequences for public subsidy of the arts. In short, why should we subsidize certain pleasures over others? Why give state support for opera but not for karaoke? It is no use arguing that some aesthetic pleasures are 'higher' since there can be no agreement that this is the case. If someone prefers Elvis to Elgar, there is no way that one can demonstrate that the pleasures provided by listening to one surpass those provided by listening to the other.

Some philosophers have attempted to demonstrate the contrary. J. S. Mill was forced to do this to defend his utilitarian morality, which viewed increasing happiness and pleasure as the greatest human goods. Critics claimed that such a morality was one for the beasts, for it would mean it was better to be a contented swine than a less happy Socrates. Mill's retort was that there were lower and higher pleasures, lower pleasures being those of the senses, such as food and sex, and higher pleasures being those of the intellect. Mill argued that 'competent judges'—those who had enjoyed both types of pleasure—would always prefer a life with some higher pleasures to one with none at all, even if the pleasures of such a life were more diluted by unhappiness or pain.

The problem for Mill is that he may be right that no human would prefer an animal life to one with 'higher' pleasures, but it does not show which of the distinctively human pleasures are superior. There are people who, having listened to both, still prefer Elvis to Elgar. To say that these people are clearly not competent judges merely begs the question. Most tellingly, it seems impossible to say that the pleasure of listening to one is superior to the other. It could be argued that Elgar is more complex and sophisticated, for example, but if someone says they enjoy the pure simplicity of Elvis's voice more, how can we say the pleasure they get from listening to him is inferior?

We could go further and argue that the existing subsidy arrangements essentially support the pleasures of the better-off as opposed to those of the less well-off. Although people of all classes enjoy the benefits of public arts subsidy, it does seem that these benefits are disproportionately enjoyed by the more wealthy. In Britain, for example, the top-priced seats at the Royal Opera House cost over £150, putting them way beyond the means of an ordinary person. Yet on average, each seat at each performance is subsidized to the tune of £40. In effect, wealthy opera-goers receive a £40 discount, courtesy of the taxpayer

As it stands, Tolstoy's argument, especially as rendered in précis here, is too crude to settle the issue. But it does, I think, issue a serious challenge that needs to be answered. If it is the state's role at all to subsidize more than essential services, why should these subsidies be directed at the cultural activities enjoyed most by the middle classes? Why shouldn't more money be spent on 'circuses' which can be enjoyed by all? I have to confess that I do not have a satisfactory answer. Though no connoisseur of art, I found myself impressed by Tate Modern and felt glad that the authorities had the boldness to deliver on its vision. Although initially intrigued, I could not muster the same enthusiasm for the Dome. The troubling question for me is whether this reflects a mere personal preference or whether or not there are compelling arguments why the one should receive public money and not the other. I would like to think there are, but wanting something to be true and it being true are two very different things.

The value of philosophy
In a chapter on value in a book about the role of philosophy I cannot resist making a small diversion to consider the value of

philosophy. Briefly, I wish to sketch out where some of its value lies, again by talking about the needs philosophy helps to satisfy.

The practical need philosophy helps meet is the need to think clearly and better. Philosophy can provide a very stringent training in what has come to be known as 'critical thinking'. Studying the structure of arguments and the nature of deduction, for example, in a highly theoretical and precise way is an excellent way of sharpening your mental skills.

Thinking philosophically helps us to draw the right conclusions from evidence. It can stop us jumping to conclusions. It helps us to decide what degree of proof or evidence is sufficient to justify accepting a conclusion. This is a very practical skill because we have to reach conclusions from evidence all the time. Indeed, we are swamped by evidence in the news media. Sometimes we have to draw our own conclusions from it. On other occasions, we have to judge whether the conclusions others have drawn are correct.

Philosophy can also help satisfy some of our intellectual needs. It is not only 'intellectuals' who have intellectual needs. We all do to a lesser or greater extent. The reason why you are reading this book is that you have some kind of need for intellectual stimulation, which I sincerely hope is being met! This is a need which sits near the top of Maslow's hierarchy, which, as we have seen, makes it in one sense extremely important indeed.

Even though the currency of philosophy is reason rather than feeling, it can still contribute towards the satisfaction of our emotional needs. Philosophy's very important role in this regard is that it can inform our emotions. Take as an example a family of emotions tied in with feelings of blame: resentment, acrimony, bitterness, and revenge. Greek tragedy addresses these emotions by means of catharsis. By observing others avenging, we are able to purge ourselves of our own feelings and satisfy a need in us which we have. Philosophy provides no such emotional outlet. But that doesn't mean it can't help us deal with these emotions.

For example, as Immanuel Kant pointed out, 'ought' implies 'can'. In other words, it cannot be said that I ought to do something unless it is possible for me to do so. It is ridiculous to say, for example, that I ought to pay off the national debt of Angola if I do not have the resources to do so. Guilt often involves a feeling that we should have done something which we did not. But if we could not do what we did not do, the idea that we ought to have done it is ridiculous. Realizing this can alleviate our feelings of guilt. So here, purely rational, philosophical reflection ends up with a change in our emotional state.

This is an example of how thought and emotion are not neatly divided aspects of life—they inform each other. People frequently report that understanding changes the way they feel. To take an example from earlier in the book, if one changes one's beliefs about the morality of Clinton's behaviour with Monica Lewinsky, it is very likely that one will change one's feelings about him. As another example, a belief that an armed conflict is justified or unjustified can make a difference to how one emotionally responds when one reads or hears news about it. Given this link between thought and feeling, it is inevitable that philosophizing will have an affect on our emotions.

The final type of need philosophy meets is the existential. What I mean by this term can be explained with an example. A young woman is trying to make up her mind about what she is going to do as she approaches her late twenties. Should she settle down, get a good, steady job, perhaps marry her boyfriend, start a family? Or should she stay young, free, and single, travel the world a bit, keep the pace of life changing? Of course, how she solves this dilemma will depend largely on what she simply happens to prefer. But in thinking about her choice, other, existential questions will also preoccupy her. Which would be the better life to live? What is life really about? Is it about preparing the next generation? Finding love? Getting your kicks? What's the point of doing any of these? These are existential questions in that they are questions about the meaning and importance of life itself. Despite popular misconceptions, a lot of philosophy has nothing at all to do with these questions. But a significant amount of it does. Again, addressing these questions is a significant need we have as persons, and if philosophy can help us to meet them, which I think it can, then philosophy meets a need.

Against all I have said, however, there needs to be weighed a major caveat. I have sketched some ways in which philosophy can help us think better and meet our intellectual, emotional, and existential needs. But I would not want to suggest that only philosophy can help us meet these needs. Indeed, there are often more direct ways of addressing them. If you're clinically depressed, don't read Plato: take Prozac and go and see a cognitive behaviourial therapist. If you want intellectual stimulation, don't confine your reading to philosophy, enjoy variety. If you want to improve your thinking skills, a course or book on critical thinking might lead to quicker results than a study of the great works of Western philosophy. The only need philosophy alone meets is the need some people have to address philosophical problems. As Wittgenstein reputedly said to Russell, 'People who like philosophy will pursue it, and others won't and there is an end of it.' If you do pursue philosophy, there are other benefits you can get from it. But it is the interest in philosophy, rather than these benefits, which should be the primary motivation.

Conclusion

Looking at the question of what has value by asking what needs something satisfies is just one way into the bigger issue of value. I would not want to give the impression that I think 'something has value if it satisfies a need' is a complete and satisfactory definition of value. It is rather a working definition which enables us to get our enquiry started. This way of looking at value has produced some interesting findings. It enables us to see how 'higher' and 'lower' needs are both important, but in different ways, which is why comparing the value of a hospital bed with an artwork like Tracey Emin's bed is so problematic. It also raises the question of why the needs of people who prefer 'high art' are met through public subsidy in preference to those who prefer middle or low-brow diversions. These considerations show how judgements like 'Dome bad, Tate Modern good', though perhaps ultimately true, are not quite as obviously true as they might appear.

It would be interesting to do a survey and to see the average length of time between someone finishing this chapter and hearing someone in the news lamenting a 'waste of taxpayers' money'. My guess is that it would be no more than a few days. What I hope to have shown here is that behind these protestations lie some difficult and complex philosophical issues surrounding the nature of value and the role of the state. Although it is an effective rhetorical device to compare the amount of money spent on something which satisfies our 'higher' needs with something that satisfies our lower ones, such direct comparisons are crass and simplistic. The full gamut of our human needs must be satisfied, not just those of existence. Nothing that meets any of these needs is without value.

The question of which needs the state should satisfy is also a thorny one. I do not have any easy answers to this, but I do think we need to question the rationale behind the set of priorities currently inherited, and we also need to be aware that the news coverage in this area may be skewed by the perceptions the news makers have of their own needs. We need health, art, and circuses. Recognizing that each has its value but that these values are not easily compared is a vital first step to any sensible discussion of government subsidy.

9

From conception to coffin: When to end life

Legal death

'We find it astounding—we can't see how it's a basic human right to be starved and dehydrated to death.' Such was the reaction of Phyllis Bowman, campaign director of Right To Life, to the news on 6 October 2000 that the British High Court had ruled in favour of doctors who wanted to stop feeding two women in a persistent vegetative state (PVS), by request of their relatives. PVS is a condition where the patient has complete unawareness of self and environment, but enough basic biological functioning for the body to stay alive if fed artificially and given medical attention. Nineteen days after the ruling, it was announced that both women, known only as Mrs H. and Mrs M., had 'died peacefully'.

The law courts had ruled similarly before, setting a precedent in 1993 when they allowed doctors to stop feeding Tony Bland, a young man left in a PVS after the Hillsborough football stadium disaster. The significance of the 2000 case was that the Human Rights Act had just been passed, incorporating the European Convention on Human Rights into British Law. The Human Rights Act guarantees everyone's right to life, which made campaigners such as Right To Life optimistic that they could show such actions by doctors to be a deprivation of a basic human right. They failed.

Two months earlier, across the Atlantic, the US president, George Bush, gave the go-ahead for a limited use of federal funds for embryonic stem-cell research. This was in spite of a campaign promise not to spend taxpayer dollars on research that would require the destruction of embryos. It was also in spite of a move made earlier that same year to reimpose a ban

placed by Ronald Reagan on US government funding for international aid groups that promote or offer abortion or abortion
counselling. A White House spokesman explained, 'The president does not support using taxpayers' funds to provide
abortions.'

The connection between these news stories is that, in each
case, there is a strong disagreement of opinion about when it is
right or permissible to kill or allow to die. On the one side, the
so-called 'pro-life' lobby argues that it is always wrong to take a
human life or allow a human to die unnecessarily, and that
human life begins at conception and ends only with biological
death. This has the merits of being a clear, simple—perhaps too
simple—and easily comprehensible position. Opponents of this
view take the line that human life is not worth preserving at all
costs and that certain forms of human life, such as the early
embryo, do not have the same value as fully developed ones.

It is easy to see why the issue is a particularly emotive one.
For 'pro-life' campaigners, abortion and allowing patients in a
PVS to die constitute literal acts of murder. This can motivate
people to take militant action to defend what they see as the
rights of those too weak to defend themselves. For example, on
22 October 1998, a sniper shot and killed Barnett Slepian, an
abortion doctor in Buffalo, New York. Such violence is sadly not
isolated. In the other camp, people believe that the right of
women to have abortions is a fundamental liberty and the keeping alive of people in a PVS by all means necessary an affront to
human dignity (and a terrible waste of health service
resources).

There is a major philosophical issue at the heart of this

debate about the value of human life. We all of us agree, I hope, that human life is ordinarily of great value, if not in some way sacred. But as these news stories show, there is great disagreement about if and when this value is to be found at the start of life and, if we lose our normal capacities, at the end of it.

There are several ways of approaching this issue philosophically. The route I am going to take is to consider the fundamental question of what a person is. To start with, then, I need to introduce a vital and contested distinction between a person and a human being.

Speciesism

At first sight, the distinction between a person and a human being might appear to be a specious one. After all, aren't all human beings persons and all persons human beings? Many philosophers have thought otherwise, including John Locke, who recounts an apocryphal tale of a talking parrot. This parrot did not just repeat phrases; it was capable of intelligent discourse, just like a human being. Locke's point was that, if such a parrot existed, wouldn't it be correct to say that it was in an important sense a person? A person in this sense is 'A thinking intelligent being that has reason and reflection and can consider itself as itself, the same thinking thing in different times and places'. On such a view, the parrot would be a person. If this seems too outrageous, consider the case of a human-like alien such as Doctor Spock. Surely we would say that Spock was a person?

The reason this distinction is vital is that the fact that something is a person has 'normative' consequences—that is to say, it affects questions of value and ethics. Normally, we do not grant the same rights to parrots as we do to humans. But if we did have a parrot such as the one Locke described, surely it would be as morally wrong to take its life without good reason as it would to kill a human being. The Human Rights Act should grant Doctor Spock the same protections as humans, even though he is not a human. (Pedantic 'Trekies' may point out here that Spock is half-human. It doesn't matter—we need only imagine what would be the case if he were fully non-human.) Not to extend these rights to non-human persons would be an example of what Richard Ryder called 'speciesism': the discrimination against something purely on the grounds of species membership. This form of discrimination is as intellectually unjustified as racism or sexism.

Because people often scoff at the phrase 'speciesism', citing it as an example of that old cliché 'political correctness gone mad', it is worthwhile clarifying what this means. It does not mean that if we ever treat other species differently to humans we are guilty of unjustified discrimination. The point is that, if we do treat them differently, that must be because of some ethically relevant difference between these other species and humans. One might try to argue that such ethically relevant differences exist between humans and all animals (although such a case is harder to make with many primates). This would justify treating animals and humans differently. The key point of introducing the concept of speciesism is to make it clear that *species membership alone* is not enough to justify this differential treatment.

This is because mere species membership is at most ethically rather unimportant and possibly entirely irrelevant. Spock too has 'human' rights.

There are two very clear consequences of accepting this line of argument. The first is that, since species membership is not itself ethically significant, it should not be in virtue of us being humans that we grant things such as human rights. The second is that, since being a person is ethically significant, as we can see by considering the ethical implications of accepting that Spock and the parrot would be persons, this is something we have to take account of when considering ethical questions about the value of a life. (The other major factor usually considered ethically important is whether a being can feel pain or not. But because that in itself is not enough for most people to justify extending full human rights to beings that can feel pain like fish or spiders, I will not consider this factor in detail here.)

The implications of accepting this for the news stories we have looked at are striking. In none of the cases is a person, as defined by Locke, being killed or allowed to die. Neither the early embryo nor the person in a persistent vegetative state is a 'thinking intelligent being that has reason and reflection and can consider itself as itself, the same thinking thing in different times and places'. The mere fact that they are human beings should not be taken to be ethically significant, or at least not ethically crucial. If this is true, then there is a very large difference between murder and allowing PVS patients to die or destroying embryos.

That is not to say that there are not other important factual and ethical questions to consider. Most notably, there is the thorny issue of diagnosis of PVS. Much is made by 'pro-life' campaigners of instances of people recovering from PVS. In almost all such cases, it turns out that doctors never claimed that the PVS was irreversible and had merely estimated a low probability of recovery. But even if mistakes have been made, the argument that PVS patients should be kept alive because we can't be sure their condition is irreversible is very different from the argument that we should keep them alive because to end their lives early is always a form of murder.

The argument of this section has been brisk and obviously more has to be said to defend its conclusions and its premises. In order to fill out the argument, it is necessary to go into more depth about what a person is. One way to get into this question is to consider the question of personal identity: what is required for a person to continue to exist as that same person? If we understand what is required for a person to continue to exist we will understand better what a person essentially is. For example, if we need our brains to survive in order to continue to exist, that would suggest that, whatever we are, we are not immaterial 'souls'.

Although we obviously change over time, we all know what it means to say, come each birthday, that this is one more anniversary in the life of one person. But what is it that makes these events in the life of one person? There are three main candidates for an adequate answer to this question. The first I will term Soul Matters. On this view, we each of us have some immaterial soul and this soul is the seat of the self. The second I will call Body Matters. On this view, we are the individual persons we are because we are individual biological animals. Our continued survival requires the continued existence of this body, or at least enough of it. The third contender is Mind Matters. On this view, being a person is being the subject of a mental life. This is broadly the view of Locke, outlined above, and is the view I wish to defend. To do this, we need to consider the failings of the other two views.

Soul Matters

The idea that we are embodied souls is a popular one and the orthodox view of many religions. Believing this to be true is one of the main motivations for many in the 'pro-life' movement. The reason why many think that George Bush is right not to spend federal money on abortions and wrong to allow stem-cell research is that the soul enters the body at the moment of conception. From that moment on, we are full individuals whose lives have intrinsic value. The reason why it is wrong to allow a person in a PVS to die is that their soul still resides in them, only leaving the body at the point of death. (Why it is so wrong to free the soul from the body early, given that it can do no more on earth, is not so easily explained.)

We could try to argue that the soul does not exist. But another strategy is to argue that even if it did exist, it could not be the seat of the self as has widely been believed. To see why this is so, consider this thought experiment, adapted and updated from Locke. If souls exist, then reincarnation is at least a possibility: if souls can both reside in or out of bodies, there is no reason why in principle they should not inhabit a series of bodies. What if reincarnation did take place and I were to reveal to you that you are the reincarnation of a fourteenth-century cobbler called

Harold? The same soul that was embodied in him resides in you. Let us go further and say that this soul has some causal role in making you who you are, shaping your character and talents. Does it follow from this that you are the same person as Harold? It does not seem that you are. The reason is that to be Harold seems to require a continuity of mental life between Harold's life and yours. With no awareness or memory of Harold's life, whatever happened in his life just wouldn't seem to be part of your life. Harold seems to be a totally different person. You may have got some abilities and some of your character from him, but that doesn't make you him. After all, we often believe we get some of our talents and character from our parents—it doesn't mean we *are* our parents.

It is important to see that what Locke offers here is not so much an argument but what Daniel Dennett calls an 'intuition pump'. That is to say, the thought experiment is a kind of device for making plain what our deepest intuitions are so that we can see the rational consequences of accepting or rejecting them. It thus serves the vital philosophical function of making things clearer, which is at least as important in philosophy as offering proofs or demonstrations.

The plausibility that the soul is the seat of the self also lessens if you think about the way in which being a particular person depends upon the way in which we are embodied, organic animals. It does not seem to be just an incidental feature of my existence that I use language, read, hear, interact with people, feel hunger, have sexual desires, and so on. It is not clear how the life of a disembodied soul could in any way resemble this kind of life. But then, if being a particular embodied person with a sense of self, memories, and so on is essential to a person being the person they are, why should we think that a person is essentially some non-material entity that can be separated from the body?

One final doubt about souls is that all the evidence we have is that we are, in fact, complex biological organisms. Consciousness is still a mystery, but our mental lives do seem to depend entirely on our being embodied humans with brains. Knock out part of the brain and you knock out language. If your brain doesn't produce enough serotonin, you will be miserable. Stimulate a certain area of the brain and everything seems funny. My consciousness and my sense of self do seem vital to me being who I am. But all this seems to depend entirely on my having a brain in an all too mortal human body.

This is an important point, which is worth stressing. Many things are not understood about the brain and consciousness. There are also many philosophical problems in simple materialist claims such as that mental states just are brain states. But these major difficulties should not be used as a means of avoiding what few philosophers or scientists seriously deny—that mental processes such as thought and feeling owe their existence to a functioning, organic brain. The relationship between brains and minds is not properly understood, but the dependence of minds on brains is rarely disputed.

The existence of souls is therefore both unlikely and irrelevant to the question of what makes us the individual persons we are. The evidence, such as it is, is very much that souls do not exist. Even if they do, it is clear that it is as conscious, human animals that we gain a sense of our individuality and selves. The soul is just irrelevant.

Body Matters

The importance of our embodied, organic nature might lead us to consider whether we would be best to think of persons just as individual human animals. One problem with this has already been discussed: if we conflate the idea of a person with that of a human, we are confusing issues of species membership with what gives our lives the value that they have. A way of dealing with this is to say that, though there may be non-human persons, human persons just are individual, human organisms.

The main problem with this view is that survival of the body (which includes the brain) seems to be neither necessary nor sufficient for survival of the individual person. In science fiction stories such as *Invasion of the Body Snatchers*, for example, we have no trouble in accepting that, though the bodies live on, once taken over by the aliens, they are no longer the bodies of their original owners. So the continued existence of the body is not sufficient to guarantee the survival of a person. Similarly, in Kafka's *Metamorphosis*, we have the horror of a person continuing to exist even though their human body is replaced by that of a beetle. In this instance, the continued existence of the human body is not necessary to the continued existence of the person. Of course, these are mere fictions, but the story writers seem to be plugging into a deep-seated belief that continued existence of our bodies is neither necessary nor sufficient to guarantee personal survival. And the fact that the fictions are coherent suggests there is no logically necessary identity between a particular body and a particular mental life.

These intuitions are strengthened when we consider how current technology might conceivably extend. People already have synthetic body parts. These include heart valves and limbs. It is not so difficult to imagine, over time, it becoming possible to replace all parts of the body with synthetic alternatives, including the brain. Imagine one person who has 2 per cent of their body replaced by synthetic parts every year for fifty years. By the end, this person would be entirely non-human. This must be true, because human is a biological category, and if one is no longer a particular type of biological organism, one can no longer be a human. Yet we would surely say—assuming the replacements had been successful—that this was the same person, in the same way as a contemporary who had lived the same lifespan without any such replacements would be the same person.

If this is true then it cannot be the case that our survival as persons depends upon the continued existence of a particular human body. And this means that it is not in virtue of being particular human organisms that we are the individual persons we are.

Mind Matters

The rejections of both Soul Matters and Body Matters rested upon an acceptance that what is really required for a person to continue to exist is that there is a continuity of mental life. Describing exactly in what this consists is not easy, but for present purposes it is enough to say that it normally comprises the kind of mental continuity we normally have in life. In many ways, I have changed over, say, the last ten years. But because there is a continuity of mental life, marked by memories, dispositions, opinions, beliefs, and so on, which change gradually but always have a connection with the past, it is correct to say that I am the same person as I was then. So although we could say that in one sense 'I am a different person from who I used to be', the fact that this 'I' is rightly taken to refer to the same person shows that what we are really talking about is the fact that one person has *changed*; not that one person has become or *changed into* another.

The Body Matters view does have something right. It does seem that a particular person can only continue to exist if they are embodied in the same kind of way. I do find it hard to make sense of a disembodied self. I am also persuaded that it is not just incidental to who one is whether or not someone is male or female. But the fact that one must be embodied in a certain way to continue to exist does not mean that being a particular person requires having a particular body. I need *a* body to continue to exist, one like this one, but not necessarily actually this one. Of course, in practice, I can only continue to exist if *this* body continues to exist. But this limitation could conceivably be removed by technology.

If we return to our news stories, we can see what the implications of this view are. Consider early embryos first. These should not be considered as little persons. Even as human beings, they are as yet not fully developed. On the Mind Matters view I have been defending, the fact that these embryos could be considered to be members of our species is irrelevant to the question of whether they have the same value as persons. The same is true of any supposed fact that they have souls, though here the only reasons we could have for believing this to be true come from religious conviction, not evidence or reason. From this it does not follow that they have no value whatsoever. But the case must be made to show why they have value and what kind of value they have. It is hard to see how any such argument could lead to the conclusion that the destruction of such embryos is the equivalent of the destruction of a person.

What of the cases of persistent vegetative state? If we accept Mind Matters, and the PVS is irreversible, these women, as persons, had already ceased to exist. The fact that they continue to exist as living human beings is, if not morally irrelevant, then at least much less morally important. If they are no longer persons and the diagnosis that they can never recover consciousness is correct, then their lives as persons have already ended.

More matters

Although I have defended the view that Mind Matters, it has to be accepted that this does have some uncomfortable consequences. For example, does it mean in cases of severe senile dementia that the old person has in a sense died and that the ill person suffering the dementia is someone else? Does it mean that when someone suffers brain damage, remembers nothing of their former life, and changes their personality that someone died when the brain damage occurred?

It is a necessary part of accepting Mind Matters that one accepts that mental continuity is not all or nothing. One may have the normal amount of mental continuity, increasingly less, and then none at all. Clearly, if I suffer selective amnesia, forgetting, say, five years of my life, I do not cease to be me. But it does not follow that I could lose all mental continuity with my past and still be me. We are dealing here with the problem I discussed in Chapter 2, where there is a clear difference at two ends of a continuum but only a grey area in between. The question anyone committed to Mind Matters must ask is 'How much mental continuity is required for survival?' whilst at the same time accepting that no hard-and-fast answer can be given. This is perhaps one issue where judgement is unavoidable. Whether in any particular case of dementia or brain damage the original person no longer exists is something we cannot decide by preset rules. It should be noted in support of Mind Matters, though, that some people whose relatives suffer extreme dementia or brain damage do feel that the person they once knew has in a very real sense already died.

Even if we do judge that a person has effectively died in such cases, that does not mean we immediately lose all respect for the life of the poor person still living in that body. We are as much governed by sentiment in these cases as we are by reason. I can only begin to imagine what my reactions would be if someone I loved suffered such a tragedy. I am sure that no matter how rationally convinced I was that my loved one had effectively ceased to exist, my emotional attachment to them would leave me determined to make sure the person who they became was treated with respect and was taken care of. I say this as someone who is perhaps more influenced by intellectual concerns than average and is not particularly sentimental. If this is how I would react, I think we need not fear how humanity as whole would. Sentiment can cloud our judgement but it is also essential to our humanity. Without human sentiment there would be nothing to motivate us to reason. In order to do anything at all, physical or mental, we must first have desires and wants. As Hume famously said, 'reason is and ought only to be the slave of the passions'.

But perhaps the biggest worry people have concerns the difficulty of judging whether a person really is thinking in the same way 'inside'. We have the horror, for example, of turning off the life-support machine of someone who has been diagnosed as being in a PVS, but is really aware of all we are saying, and is internally crying out not to be killed. Two points can be made here. First, the question of *how we can tell* mental continuity has ceased is quite distinct from the general question of whether mental continuity *is necessary* for survival. We may believe that Mind Matters is the correct view, but also believe that no person is in a position to judge of another person whether there is mental continuity or not. In other words, no action follows inevitably from accepting Mind Matters. The second point is that, horror stories notwithstanding, there are at least some cases where we can know beyond all reasonable doubt that a person has irretrievably lost consciousness. It is a horrible thought, but there are no cases of someone recovering consciousness after having either their brain stem totally destroyed or their brains effectively turning to liquid. We should not use a few examples of incredible recoveries from comas as evidence that there is no such thing as irreversible brain death.

Quality of life

Opponents of the 'pro-life' lobby often try to argue that it is not life in itself which is sacred, but that the quality of life has to be taken into account. There is something in this argument of merit, particularly when it comes to cases of voluntary euthanasia. Many terminally ill people wish to have medical help to kill themselves painlessly before their lives become, in their own view, unbearable. Voluntary euthanasia remains illegal everywhere except Holland, where the Senate approved a law to legalize the practice in April 2001. In such instances, there does seem to be a strong case to be made that, if an individual judges that their quality of life is no longer acceptable, and that there is no chance of it improving, then they should have the freedom to end that life as painlessly as possible.

Many 'pro-lifers' will reject quality of life arguments. Some will do so because they hold that human life is sacred, whatever its quality. Your life can be a hell on earth, but it is still wrong to end it. Others will argue that it is not for us to judge the quality of other people's lives. Indeed, how can anyone have the presumption to judge of another being that its quality of life is such that it is not worth keeping alive? In the case of abortion, it will also be pointed out that there is every chance the embryo will have a good quality of life, if it is allowed to come to maturity. This latter point is particularly hard to refute. Abortions are often carried out when the parents lack the financial means or family set-up to bring up the child properly, or where it is in some way disabled. But unless we are to say that children from poor or broken homes and the physically disabled do not have lives worth living, we cannot use their *future* quality of life as a sufficient justification for an abortion.

But in the cases of embryo research and PVS, the issue is not one of *quality* of life. Rather it is one of what *kind* of life there is.

Consider the case of the early embryo, which George Bush is so keen to protect. Here, one cannot even talk about quality of life. Until the embryo has become more developed and has some kind of consciousness, it can have no more quality of life than a tree or a stone. So it is not that the foetus does not have a sufficiently good quality of life, it is rather that it is not yet the kind of being where it is even appropriate to talk about quality of life. It is also true that the person in a PVS, lacking all consciousness, has no quality of life. It is not that they have a poor quality of life; they do not have the kind of life which can have a quality at all.

This is why the case of voluntary euthanasia is very different from that of abortion and the care of patients in a PVS. Although for 'pro-life' activists the issue is the same in all three—it is always wrong to take a human life—those who disagree have to do so on different grounds. Voluntary euthanasia is about what a person should or should not be allowed to do with her own life. The treatment of embryos and people in a PVS is about whether or not a person actually exists or not.

Conclusion

In this chapter, as in the others, there is plenty to be said against what I have argued. In particular, many philosophers have argued that arguments about abortion and patients in a PVS do not hinge upon questions about whether the embryo or a PVS patient are persons or not. I remain unconvinced. It seems to me that the reason why the British High Court was right to allow Mrs H. and Mrs M. to be left to die is that they were no longer, in Locke's terms, thinking intelligent beings capable of considering themselves as themselves. That's just another way of saying they were no longer persons. This must surely be the central issue, for if they had been thinking intelligent beings capable of considering themselves as themselves, there could have been no justification in depriving them of food and water without their consent. The same is true of early embryos. If such embryos were thinking intelligent beings capable of considering themselves as themselves, abortion and research of stem cells taken from such embryos would not be justified. It is the fact that they are not persons which makes both abortion and the research ethically acceptable.

These issues are not going to go away. In the United States in particular, the 'pro-life' lobby has been encouraged ever since President Bush made that first announcement of ending of federal aid for overseas groups promoting or advising on abortion. We are going to read more about the sanctity of human life and the dangers of 'playing God'. Extremely emotive arguments are going to be used to sway our opinions. Having a firm, rationally defensible idea of what a person is and why it has value is going to be essential to make sense of this acrimonious and deeply felt debate.

10

The rest of life: Philosophy beyond the headlines

The rest of life

There are two conflicting ways of viewing philosophy. Expressing one view, A. J. Ayer is reported to have said that 'There's philosophy and there's the rest of life'. The alternative view is that philosophy infuses all of life. One cannot engage in it in a vacuum. Any serious philosopher must be capable of making connections between their reflections concerning one question and their attitudes and beliefs over another. Our beliefs form an interlinking network and nothing can be considered in complete isolation.

There is a certain kind of philosophy which it is perhaps possible to separate out from the rest of life. These are its most abstract and theoretical branches. Logic, high-level philosophy of language, and the philosophy of mathematics might fall into this category. But for the kind of philosophy that has been discussed in this book, it seems truer to say that it exists within the whole of life, not separated from it. If one is serious about considering current affairs through the lens of philosophy, one should expect one's broader vision to be affected and that there will be an ongoing interplay between our philosophical beliefs, our general outlook, and what the news tells us. Taking a more philosophical attitude to the news should have an affect beyond how we understand current affairs.

This means living a more philosophical life, by which I mean a life where we use and develop our powers of critical thinking, informed by the insights and arguments of philosophers, to examine the ideas, arguments, and options which we confront. I want to use this final chapter to explore some of the aspects of this life and what its adoption entails.

Because this might sound rather high-faluting I am particularly keen that certain misconceptions about the philosophical life are also set to one side. It is not primarily about developing one's own 'philosophy of life'. A philosophy of life can range from a simple maxim one always follows ('live for today'; 'Don't do anything you wouldn't want your mother to know about', etc.) to a complex view of life's purpose or meaning. Of course, philosophy can lead us to these things, but that is not what a large amount of philosophy is about. Many who focus only on these aspects of philosophy end up neglecting the important analytic side of philosophy in favour of its more speculative features. Our goals should be to develop clear thinking about these questions. Sound conclusions are more likely to follow if we prioritize good reasoning. They are less likely to follow if we prioritize finding a final answer. In our hurry, we are more likely to build our castles on erroneous sand.

Nor is living a philosophical life generally about developing a theory which explains the fundamental nature of reality and human life. Many attempts to do this are essentially no more than plausible-sounding speculations. The danger is that we come up with some ideas and are bedazzled by the creations of our own minds. We feel we have had an important insight and we soon get to work constructing our beloved theory. What then happens is that we get so attached to our theory that we find ourselves committed to it and no longer subjecting it to rational scrutiny. The idea becomes something to nurture and protect. When this happens, we have ceased to be philosophers. The philosopher should be committed to discovering the truth by clear thinking, not to defending his own ideas come what may. However, to do so requires courage, for several reasons.

First of all, it is a depressing thought, but very few of us have any entirely original ideas. (I'm sure I have not been blessed with any.) If, for example, you've thought that time could run in a circle, you can be sure that many others have too. What is more, the idea has also been subjected to great scrutiny by minds often equal or superior to our own. If we sit in our studies, building our theories while paying no attention to what others have contributed to the subject, then we risk making the same mistakes others have made. So rather than setting out to complete our pet theories in isolation, we should always attempt to seek out the contributions of other thinkers. Almost always, we will discover that they have already examined our ideas in more depth than we could do alone in one lifetime. In the short term, that may be depressing, but in the long run, only good can come of it. We may discover we were just wrong. There's no joy in that, but at least it prevents us from believing a falsehood. We may discover we were on the right tracks, but that the theory has been more developed by others. What we then come to believe will not be our own theory, but what it lacks in 'mine-ness' it gains in truth and completeness. And there is always the possibility that we can build yet further on the work of others. I think any of these possibilities is preferable to developing a philosophy of life which is one's own but inferior.

What this example also shows is the importance of dialogue in philosophy. In general, we are not very good at seeing what is wrong with our own reasoning. It must be remembered that even single-author philosophy books have usually been scrutinized by peers and revised, often several times, as a result. We are much more likely to make progress if we can discuss our ideas with other philosophically minded people. This is psychologically tough at times. It is not always fun having one's ideas constantly challenged. But it is only by responding to such challenges that our ideas really develop. This is why the image of the philosopher in the garret alone in thought is a misleading one. From the time of Socrates, arguing in the streets, through the academy of Plato, the lyceum of Aristotle, and the modern university, philosophers have always relied on contact with fellow thinkers to sharpen their skills and hone their arguments. Nowadays, this engagement can also come through the internet or, to a limited extent, by reading books. The important thing is that we get it from somewhere.

So a philosophical approach to life is not about developing a philosophy of life, nor about constructing one's own metaphysical system in the privacy of one's own mind. It is rather about subjecting all our beliefs to clear, rational scrutiny, including our beliefs about what constitutes clear, rational thinking. This is something best done in conjunction with others, not just by ourselves, which is why philosophers sometimes come across as such argumentative souls. Whereas often our conversations tend to be really no more than exchanges of ideas, the philosopher wants to examine these ideas and probe them more. To those unfamiliar with this approach, such scrutiny can seem like a challenge or a threat. But the aim is not to quarrel, it is to pursue the truth.

The miserable philosopher

This kind of life may sound very noble and attractive, but there are those who think that one can be too philosophical. One reason is that some people think that philosophy makes you miserable. We all know about existentialists, who wear black, talk about anguish, abandonment, and despair and end up killing themselves. We know about Nietzsche, driven mad by philosophy. And we know about Kierkegaard, as gloomy a soul as you could imagine. And who can blame them? The more you examine life the less it seems to make sense. Better to forget philosophy and just get on with things.

The problem with such a view is that it is founded on anecdote and myth. It would be hard to show if thinking philosophically made people more or less happy. Even if it were discovered in general philosophers were unhappier than non-philosophers, the question would still remain as to whether unhappy people are drawn to philosophy or whether it is the philosophy which makes them unhappy.

In the absence of sound research, we can only go on the available evidence. The examples cited above of miserable philosophers, for example, are not quite what they seem. First of all, it is interesting to note that all the anecdotes concern existentialism, so at the very best they would stand as evidence that existentialism makes you unhappy, not philosophy as a whole. However, even this does not stand up to scrutiny. Take Nietzsche. That he was sent mad by his philosophy fits the tragic-romantic stereotype of the existentialist hero, but not the facts. Nietzsche was sent mad by syphilis, which he is presumed to have contracted from an Italian prostitute in what was believed to be an almost unique diversion from an otherwise celibate life. Syphilis can infect the nervous system, and so it is almost certain that Nietzsche's madness was brought on not by philosophy, but biology. The moral of the story is to steer clear not of philosophy, but of sexually transmitted diseases.

As for Kierkegaard, to blame philosophy is again to mistake the symptom for the disease. Kierkegaard's father was, as they termed it in those days, a melancholic, who believed his family were doomed to be punished as retribution for the time he cursed God on Jutland Heath. By the time he was 21, four of Kierkegaard's siblings and his mother had died. So whichever way you stand on the nature/nurture debate, Kierkegaard was always likely to turn out a depressive. And indeed, the auto-biographical evidence very much suggests that it was his personality which drove him to philosophy, not philosophy which drove him to depression.

The image of existentialism as a whole is also misleading. Sartre, for example, though he did indeed talk about anguish, abandonment, and despair, also claimed that existentialism is the most optimistic philosophy of all, as it asserts the absolute freedom of people to create for themselves the life they desire. Certainly, existentialism in the popular imagination was a gloomy, depressing, pointless doctrine, but we cannot blame philosophy for the misinterpretations of fashionable black-clad youths.

What tends to get less attention are the many cases of philosophers who, if not always jolly, report on the positive effects of their philosophical life. There is Socrates, who is reported to have greeted his death with great equanimity. This is even more surprising when one considers that he had been sentenced to death by drinking hemlock for corrupting the youth of Athens with his philosophy. Yet it was his philosophical outlook which enabled him to take things so calmly. Spinoza (one recent biography notably excepting) is also reputed to have been a well-adjusted, contented person. Stuart Hampshire, in his book on the Dutch rationalist, wrote, 'He had the reputation of being a man of great courtesy and amenity, and among his neighbours he seems to have been loved and respected; he was certainly not dour, dull or disapproving.' Another cheery fellow was David Hume. Adam Smith said of him that 'His temper, indeed, seemed to be more happily balanced, if I may be allowed such an expression, than that perhaps of any other man I have ever known'. And Hume's doctor, writing of his death to Adam Smith, noted that in his last days 'he never dropped the smallest expression of impatience; but when he had occasion to speak to the people about him, always did it with affection and tenderness'.

So the anecdotal evidence is inconclusive and certainly shows there is no inevitable link between a bleak view of the world and living a philosophical life. Bertrand Russell has suggested something even more positive: that philosophy actually contributes to a more serene view on life. In *The Problems of Philosophy*, he compares the non-reflective, instinctive life with the reflective, 'philosophic' one:

The life of the instinctive man is shut up within the circle of his private interests: family and friends may be included, but the outer world is not regarded except as it may help or hinder what comes within the circle of instinctive wishes. In such a life there is something feverish and confined, in comparison with which the philosophic life is calm and free.

Russell is suggesting that philosophy enables us to see the broader picture, and in doing so, it enables us to free ourselves from the claustrophobic concerns of day-to-day life. I think there is something in what Russell says, even though the argument is made less persuasive by the fact that Russell himself hardly lived a serene life. But it does seem to me that people who are too wrapped up in their own lives and problems also tend to be the most dissatisfied, the most complaining, and the most difficult to be with. Seeing the broader picture is, as Russell describes it, like being able to breathe more easily in the open space.

I would therefore—with some hesitation as the evidence is inconclusive—suggest that more often than not, a more philosophical approach to life is at least as likely to contribute to greater contentment and serenity than it is to make you miserable. Obviously, the good life contains a variety of different things. In advocating the philosophical life, I am only saying that philosophical thought can be a valuable component in the good life, not its sole ingredient. Also, philosophy is not for everyone—some just don't feel any urge to question as philosophers do and it would perhaps be harmful to try to make them act against their nature. But for many, probably the majority, I think we have reason to believe it can contribute to our satisfaction with life.

Thought versus action

There is, however, a second objection to the philosophical life, and that is that reflection tends to decrease action. In other words, the more we think about things the less we actually get done. As Hamlet soliloquized:

> And thus the native hue of resolution
> Is sicklied o'er with the pale cast of thought.

This reminds me of the famous Monty Python sketch, where a team of German philosophers play a team of Greek philosophers at football. When the whistle is blown to start the match, instead of kicking the ball, all the players walk around, stroking their beards. Such is the stereotype of the impractical philosopher.

As Hamlet is often taken to be a case study in how thinking prevents action, let us look at what the real lessons of *Hamlet* are. There is, in fact, a good case to be made that Hamlet was right to think before launching into his revenge. First of all, remember that Hamlet is told of his father's murder by the visitation of a ghost. We would hardly think it advisable behaviour for someone to murder solely on the basis that they'd seen a ghost who had told them to do so. Hamlet, therefore, sets about trying to confirm whether or not the ghost's claims are true. To do so, he hatches a plan to present the king—the alleged murderer—with a play that parallels the alleged murder of his father. The king's reaction to the play confirms the ghost's story, and Hamlet is then resolved to seek his revenge.

Hamlet's lack of action is thus commendable. It is simply not true that the best thing to do is always to act first and think later. In fact, in many of Shakespeare's other plays, we see the tragic consequences of acting on hearsay or prima facie evidence without seeking to establish whether it is true or not. The tragedy of Othello is that he falls for the deceit of Iago. If only he had, like Hamlet, thought a bit more and tried to establish for himself whether or not Desdemona had really been unfaithful. And in *Romeo and Juliet*, if only Romeo had stopped to check if Juliet were really dead before taking his own life! (That would have been the Hollywood ending.) In *Hamlet*, the irony is that the one time Hamlet acts without thinking first, he actually ends up killing the wrong man, Polonius. This unreflective action is what leads to the plot by Laertes and the King to kill Hamlet, and the blood-bath that is the play's final scene.

On the evidence of the Bard, therefore, thinking less and act-ing more is a disastrous policy. Of course, if our only evidence for this were *The Complete Works of Shakespeare*, the case would be incomplete. But I think it is easy to see how the principle is mirrored in life. For example, it is often noted that many bad laws are enacted when they are hurried through Parliament in reaction to recent events. The less reflection and rational scru-tiny a bill receives, the more likely the resultant law is a bad or unworkable one. On a more domestic note, the old refrain, 'marry in haste, repent at leisure' strikes a chord. The point is simply that there's no virtue in acting unless one acts correctly. Better to do nothing at all than act and make things worse.

The other point to remember is that, despite the Monty Python sketch, philosophers do not stop and think before doing everything. Philosophers must learn not only *how* to think, but also *when* the appropriate time for thought is. We know the philosophically inclined don't pause for thought in a football match. Nor do they stop and consider whether the fire is real if caught in a burning building—they get out. Philosophical think-ing has a role to play in life, but that does not mean it must dominate all aspects of life. Only in parodies do philosophers always think where what is really needed is action.

There are even times when the fact that one tends to think about things more than is usual can actually make one more, not less, decisive. For example, consider the case where you are buying a bicycle and are about to pay and realize for some reason that the bicycle is, in fact, stolen. Perhaps you notice that there is a security code which has been filed away. What do you do? You could act instinctively. If you did this, it is very possible—perhaps 50/50, that you will make a decision which on reflection you feel was wrong. You could try to work out the morally correct thing to do, which would lead to indecision and uncertainty while you make up your mind. But had you previously considered the morality of buying stolen goods, which the philosophically inclined person is likely to have done, you would be more able to make a quick decision which you would later feel comfortable with. In this example, a philosophical approach to life can actually help us to make better, quicker decisions when put on the spot.

This is why the notion of character is so central to the philosophy of Aristotle. He recognized that we are essentially creatures of habits. One job of philosophy, he thought, was to determine those aspects of our character that we need to cultivate. The actual cultivation of these traits occurs through behaviour and habit. In this way we can see how rational thought can guide us in those parts of life where it is not actually deployed.

A final thing to consider on the topic of action is that a well-rounded philosopher will also learn when it is better to act not on the basis of reason, but on instinct or 'gut feeling'. As I have already suggested, philosophy does not and should not override the survival instinct that makes us flee fires and dodge traffic. In addition to this, we all have at least some aspect of our lives where our non-reflective judgement is better than our reflective one, or is at the very least more likely to provide an accurate judgement quicker. For example, if experience shows you are good at 'sniffing out' a bad deal, then you would be wise to follow your instinct even if, rationally, you cannot see what is wrong with it. Reason plays a role here, but that role is to judge what, on the basis of experience, is a more reliable judge: instinct or reason. It is, in fact, rational to prefer instinct over reason if instinct gets it right more often than reason. It may sound odd to say it is sometimes rational to act non-rationally, but it is not strictly speaking a paradox.

Life's meaning

It's always slightly embarrassing for anyone to talk about the meaning of life, especially if you're a philosopher. It is a popular misconception that the philosopher's main task is to find out the meaning of life. In fact, it is hardly a concern for professional philosophers at all, and philosophers spend so much of their time correcting this misconception that when they actually do turn to the subject they do so a little sheepishly. Another reason for this reluctance to deal with the subject is that you can find countless books offering a 'philosophy of life' piled up in the new age and spirituality sections of bookshops, which would not be considered by most philosophers to be proper philosophy at all. This is partly because it is just different to philosophy as studied in universities and partly because the vast majority of it is quite simply appallingly argued. A third difficulty is that the question of the meaning of life is as big a question as you could ask and anyone seriously addressing it who does not suffer from a superiority complex is intensely aware of the danger of conceit.

However, the question cannot be ignored and is likely to press upon us even more if we think and reflect about world events. Who can read about poverty, disease, war, tragedy, environmental dangers and not wonder what the point of living is at all? As a means of making everything in life seem futile, following the news seems as good as any. Here again we have an example of the way in which there is an interplay between our broader ideas, philosophy, and current affairs. Each informs the other and raises questions which cut across any supposed boundaries between ourselves, our philosophizing, and our understanding of the news.

Needless to say, there is no way that I am going to claim to know the true meaning of life. What I can do is examine what the very idea of there being a meaning to life entails. Clearly the meaning of life is not like the meaning of a word or a symbol. We don't think that life is a kind of symbol that stands for something else. But another sense of 'meaning' is the wider significance something has. So when Christians talk about the 'meaning of Christmas' they are talking about the way in which Christmas is not just about presents and food, but that it commemorates the birth of Jesus, who they believe to be the son of God. Similarly, we can examine data about temperature records around the world and ask what it means. The answer, according to some, is that it means that the world is getting warmer, which in turn means that the planet faces difficulties in the future. In both these cases, 'meaning' is about the greater significance a relatively limited phenomenon has. 'What does it mean?' can be rephrased to 'What is its significance?'

It is natural that we should ask this question about our own lives, as what often worries us is the feeling that, in the grand scheme of things, our lives lack significance. To someone looking at us from space, we are like ants, each going about its business but ultimately not really mattering very much. Any one of us could die and history would not even notice. Even so-called important people suffer the same fate in the long run. The famous statue's inscription was 'My name is Ozymandias, king of kings: Look on my works, ye Mighty, and despair!' Yet the story is told not to show us how significant Ozymandias was, but as a salutary lesson in the folly of grandeur, as over time nothing remained of Ozymandias' great works but the eroding statue plinth.

Whether we can find meaning in our lives by thinking of our significance depends very much on how great a significance we can be satisfied with. If we consider our significance in the history of the universe, we will find very little. It is difficult to see how the universe as a whole would be significantly different if I had not existed. If we are looking for significance in the history of humanity, very few of us will find satisfaction there. Individuals who change the tide of history are few and far between. It is much easier to find significance in a much narrower way, exemplified in Frank Capra's feel-good movie *It's a Wonderful Life*. The film's protagonist, George, considers his life a failure.

He always dreamed of travelling and of being a big shot, but a combination of his own selflessness and bad luck conspired to keep him rooted in his own town, frustrated. He attempts suicide but is rescued by a guardian angel, who shows him all the ways in which his life has contributed to the well-being and happiness of people all around him, not in big, ostentatious ways, but just by his thought, consideration, and helpfulness. George comes to the conclusion that he hasn't been a failure at all and that his life has had a significance for all the people for whom life would have been not quite as good as it has been without him. (In our more cynical times, the film could be remade as *It's a Rotten Life*, in which the roles are reversed, and a selfish, self-satisfied oaf is driven to suicide by an angel who shows him how his significance has been purely negative and that the world would have been, in countless small ways, better without him.) There is always a friend, a parent, a sibling, or a student whose lives have been made better by us, and hopefully they outnumber those whose lives we have made worse, by accident or design. In this sense our lives can have a significance beyond themselves.

However, whether this is sufficient to give meaning to our lives is another matter. Certainly, many people do find meaning to their lives in just this way. In particular, many people find that being a parent and thus having children who need them and whose welfare depends on them, is more than enough to give meaning to their daily lives. But to others, this seems too modest. If this is the only meaning life has, it seems to them insufficient. So you care for your kids, and they their kids, and so on until humanity dies or a generation ends the line by not reproducing. In the end, the family line is just a dot in human history and matters not an iota in the grand scheme of things.

When we think of our significance in this way, we have to distinguish between the facts of the matter and how we respond to them. The facts are simply that your life has a greater significance for those immediately around you, probably virtually none for humanity as a whole, and even less for the universe as a whole. These facts reveal the extent to which your life has significance. But these facts do not tell the whole story, because the search for a meaning of life is to a large extent a personal search for something that makes us feel as individuals that our lives have a meaning. It is more than possible that while one person is satisfied by the significance his life has and has thus found a meaning to his life, others, whose lives are equally significant measured objectively, are dissatisfied and do not consider that this significance gives a meaning to their lives. It all depends on how significant you feel the need to be.

These thoughts bring out the sense in which 'the meaning of life' has a subjective element. It is easy to think of the meaning of life as some kind of secret which, once revealed, would tell everyone what their lives were for. In this sense, the meaning of life would be something objective, waiting to be discovered, and which applies to all humanity. But there is another sense in which the meaning of life is something subjective, to be found by each of us individually. The search here is for what makes my life meaningful *for me*. In this sense there is no reason to suppose that what makes one person's life meaningful for him would make another person feel his life was meaningful.

It should be noted at this point that a lot of the appeal of religion is that it tells us we are much more significant then we would otherwise have reason to believe. Christianity, for example, teaches us that God cares about each of us so much that he even knows the number of hairs on our heads. We are all of infinite value to God and so our significance is immeasurable. What could be more significant than being the joint most important thing to God?

However, even in this case, our personal reactions are very important. Certainly, for many people, being important to God is enough to give their life meaning. But others may not feel the same. They may feel that if their only significance is to God, that actually makes them feel even less valuable. You can compare it to being a slave. A slave is very unlikely to be made content by being told that his life has a meaning, namely to serve his owner. The reason for this is that it follows that the meaning of his life is entirely defined by his significance for another person. The slave's life matters, but to his master, not to himself. Similarly with God, one could feel that being of utmost significance to God is all very well, but that seems to make my life meaningful for God, not me. So even if we accept the religious view that we are all immeasurably valuable to God, it still doesn't change the fact that this only tells us the objective facts: there is still the question of whether, subjectively, these facts make our lives meaningful for us.

Meaning and purpose

There is another sense of 'meaning', which at first sight seems even more promising than the above, and that is the idea of meaning as purpose. In fact, it is very rare for us to use the word meaning to signify purpose, except in the specific context of the meaning of life. Many find it natural to think that for something to have purpose it must have been given that purpose by someone or something. The purpose of a knife, for example, is to cut. Here, the purpose can be traced back to the knife's designer or maker. The knife was made by someone in order to fulfil a certain purpose. When we talk about human life as having a purpose, it is therefore also natural to think of someone giving us this purpose. This someone or something is usually either God or the mystical forces of nature.

However, there are other ways of thinking about purpose, which do not presuppose such a creator or purpose-giver. For example, Jean-Paul Sartre argued that there is no God and thus we cannot have a purpose in the same way as a knife does. Nonetheless, we can look at our own lives and create our own purposes. I can, for example, make the creation of art my life's purpose, or it could be that I determine to fight communism or fascism. In either case, any purpose our lives have is chosen by ourselves, not by a creator or evolution.

It is important to realize that we can still talk about purpose without assuming the purpose is given to us by someone or something. If we do not, then we will assume that the idea that life has a purpose depends upon a belief in God, which it does not. In what I will go on to say about purpose, I make no assumptions about the source of whatever purpose we might have.

How might we go about exploring what the purpose of life could be? It may be helpful to follow in Aristotle's footsteps and think about the way in which the idea of purpose is explained by the relation between means and ends. For example, what is the purpose of a pen? Its purpose is to be used for writing. The pen is a means by which the end of writing is achieved. Similarly, what is the purpose of putting money into a savings account? The purpose could be to have security, or eventually to buy a car or leave an inheritance. So the saving is a means by which to achieve the end of security, a car, or an inheritance. So when we talk about life's meaning being its purpose, it seems we are saying that life is a means to some end. There is some final goal which life is a means of achieving.

What sort of thing must this goal be? A goal can be a single, one-off aim. For example, in playing a football match, the goal is to win. Once the game is won, the purpose of the match is achieved and that is the end of that. The problem is that if life is like this, then what do we do once we fulfil our purpose? It would seem there would be nothing left to do, unless there was a never-ending series of purposes to fulfil. This is not a particularly enthralling prospect. But something's purpose need not be a single, one-off goal. For example, the purpose of a knife is to cut, and it can cut again and again. All the time the knife is being used for cutting, it is fulfilling its purpose. This might appear to be a better model for purpose in human life. If our purpose is to engage in some kind of activity or task, and that is one we can do again and again, there is no danger of us reaching that point where our purpose has been fulfilled and we are left purposeless again.

Whether our goal is a single, realizable aim or to live or function in a certain way, there are reasons for believing that the goal must be something that is good in its own right, or as we might say, something intrinsically good. Something is intrinsically good if it is good for no other reason than that it is good in itself. Many, including Aristotle and Mill, would say that happiness is such an intrinsic good. There is no answer to the question, 'Why is happiness good?' Happiness just *is* a good thing. Such intrinsic goods are contrasted with instrumental goods—things that are not good in themselves, but are good because they are a means to an intrinsically good end. Many would say money can be instrumental. It is not money itself which we value, it is what we can do with it.

So if the meaning of life lies in its purpose, the goal must be something worth having in its own right. Many religions have held out the possibility of heaven as an example of such a goal. Heaven is supposed to be a place or state of mind so blissful that merely being there is reason enough to want it. What is interesting about this is that heaven so described is actually recognizable. Almost all of us know what it is to be in a state where the nature of the experience itself is what makes it worth having. Such experiences can be high-minded, such as listening to a piece of music or witnessing a beautiful sunset, or they can be more animalistic, such as the pleasures of sex and eating good food. Such experiences are good in themselves—intrinsically good, not just instrumentally good. (It should be noted that just because such experiences are intrinsically good that does not mean it is always right to have them, as they may also be instrumentally bad, and thus overall bring about more intrinsic badness than goodness. One example might be sexual infidelity, where the experience of the sex is good in itself, but the consequences lead to many more intrinsically bad states, such as unhappiness, mistrust, guilt, and bitterness.)

The appeal of heaven, therefore, lies in the fact that we already recognize what an intrinsically good state is. The difference with heaven is that whereas in life such moments are but fleeting, in heaven the state persists in perpetuity. Some would also believe that there is a qualitative difference, in that the happiness of heaven is purer and more intense than earthly happiness.

If there were such a thing as heaven, it would therefore seem to be the case that it would provide a meaning for life, in that the purpose of life could be to gain entry to heaven and thus to be able to enjoy something intrinsically good for ever. Life is the means to the end of heaven. However, fewer and fewer people believe in heaven, for various reasons, including many I discussed in Chapter 9 concerning the nature of the self. For those who do not believe such a state exists, what then could be the purpose of life? If life is to have a purpose, but that purpose is not after life, then it follows that for it to have any purpose at all, it must be found within this life. From what we have said, that must constitute the bringing about of states or the undertaking of activities which are valuable in themselves. We have already seen that we recognize what such states are. The purpose of our lives could therefore be to achieve these things. These things can vary from individual to individual. Any number of experiences can be valuable in themselves, from listening to Wagner to losing oneself in a crossword puzzle. Who can argue, for example, with the immortal lines of a cheesy 1970s pop song, 'I love to love, but my baby just loves to dance'?

This answer to the meaning of life may also seem unsatisfactory, because it still leaves us with the problem that when death comes, it is all over. It is easy to feel that life would still be ultimately meaningless because it ends in nothing. However, it is not obvious that only things which endure for ever can be truly meaningful, which is what this sentiment seems to imply. Our mortality may be regrettable, but that needn't render our lives meaningless. Nevertheless, as I have suggested, there is a subjective element to life's meaning, and if someone does not feel their life can be given meaning by filling it with intrinsically good things, then such an account of the meaning of life fails.

The philosophical person

I'd like to conclude by linking what I have said about the role of philosophy in our lives with the main theme of this book, the philosophy behind the headlines. To do this, I would like to sketch three somewhat crude stereotypes of three different kinds of person—the non-philosophical, the pseudo-philosophical, and the genuinely philosophical—and how they respond to what they see and read in the news media.

The non-philosophical person is more bounced around by what they read, see, and hear than really in control of their life. As they never step back and analyse what is going on around them, they are doomed always to be reacting to events, rather than really taking control of them. They are easily led astray by persuasive talkers, advertisers, and politicians because they have not developed the skills necessary to analyse and judge their arguments. They take some things to be true and others to be false, yet they have no clear understanding as to why they do so. Sometimes they are right and sometimes they are wrong, but which occasion is which seems largely a matter of luck.

The pseudo-philosophical person thinks they are very wise indeed. Jealously guarding their pet theories, they pity the poor souls who criticize them only because they do not understand. They read about what people in public life say only in order to pour scorn on those they disagree with and to pull apart their arguments. Such a person is happy to criticize those who get involved in current affairs, mocking them for their naive views. They feel themselves to be above the business of everyday life. They live, in many ways, in their own insulated world, coming out only to tell everyone else they're wrong and to buy groceries.

The truly philosophical person treats their own views with as much scepticism as those of the people they read about. They are always ready to subject any belief to rational scrutiny, not as a game, but in order to understand more. Their broad outlook and openness to new arguments gives their life a kind of freedom and space. They learn a sense of perspective and of humility. They also learn when thinking is appropriate and what kinds of reasoning are suited to different purposes. They do not always expect final answers, but follow Aristotle's advice to expect only that degree of precision which each subject matter allows. Nor do they dogmatically refuse to accept anything that does not have a rational explanation, but rather use rationality as a tool and guide, accepting that it cannot always do all the work. Perhaps most importantly, the information they acquire through their following of the news informs their own beliefs and opinions at least as much as their philosophical beliefs inform their understanding of the news.

Stereotypes do not describe real people but can present models to be avoided or followed. I believe that the philosophical person I have described is a positive stereotype and that if we aspire to be as much like this as possible then not only will we understand the news better, but the news will also be a source of greater understanding for our wider opinions, beliefs, and values.

Further Reading

There are many good books on philosophy that address themes discussed in this book. I restrict myself here to just a few that are good starting points.

If your interest is in philosophical approaches and methods, mine and Peter S. Fosl's *The Philosopher's Toolkit* (Oxford: Blackwell, 2002) is a comprehensive and hopefully accessible textbook on philosophical reasoning. If that has more information than you think you're ready for, Nigel Warburton's *Thinking from A to Z* (2nd edn, London: Routledge, 2000) is a concise guide to the same theme while John Shand's *Arguing Well* (London: Routledge, 2000) is small, clear, and systematic.

If your interest is in reading original philosophy classics, Nigel Warburton's anthology *Philosophy: Basic Readings* (London: Routledge, 1999) will give you many tasters that can help you find something suitable. My *Philosophy: Key Texts* (Basingstoke: Palgrave, 2002) provides systematic discussion of five classic texts by Aristotle, Descartes, Hume, Russell, and Sartre.

If you prefer a thematic rather than text-based exploration of philosophy, my *Philosophy: Key Themes* (Basingstoke: Palgrave, 2002) covers theory of knowledge, philosophy of mind, philosophy of religion, political philosophy, and ethics. Of particular relevance to *Making Sense* are political philosophy— covered excellently in Michael Rosen and Jonathan Wolff's anthology *Political Thought* (Oxford: Oxford University Press, 1999)—and ethics, for which Peter Singer (ed.), *A Companion to Ethics* (Oxford: Blackwell, 1991) is a comprehensive introduction and reference book containing many short essays on a wide variety of subjects.

For a regular shot of philosophy, consider subscribing to *The Philosophers' Magazine* (*www.philosophers.co.uk*), a quarterly I edit aimed at both specialists and general readers. Also, published three times a year, is *Think*, a paperback-book format periodical of the Royal Institute of Philosophy aimed at the general public (*www.royalinstitutephilosophy.org/think*).

Finally, for reference buy Ted Honderich's *Oxford Companion to Philosophy* (Oxford: Oxford University Press, 1995).

Illustration Sources

Chapter 1 'Bin Laden, on tape, boasts of Trade Center attacks.'
New York Times, 14 December 2001
© New York Times

Chapter 2 ' 'The truth is the truth.' But how will the American
People judge the president?' *The Guardian*,
17 August 1998
© The Guardian. Photo © Agence Presse/EPA

Chapter 3 'Bush vows to use good times for great goals.'
The Times, 4 August 2000
© Times Newspapers Limited, 2000

Chapter 4 'Bush declares all-out war on the havens of terrorism.'
Daily Telegraph, 14 September 2001
© Telegraph Group Limited, 2001. Photo
© Kevin Lamarque/Reuters

Chapter 5 'Scientists clone human embryos.' *The Times*,
26 November 2001
© Times Newspapers Limited, 2001

Chapter 6 'Peer arrested after raid on GM crop.' *The Times*,
27 July 1999
© Photo © Greenpeace/Steve Morgan

Chapter 7 'Sit back and wait until you see God.' *Daily Mirror*,
20 April 1993
© Mirror Syndication International

Chapter 8 'Scandal of the dome.' *Sunday Mirror,*
10 September 2000
© Mirror Syndication International

Chapter 9 'Allow these women to die with dignity, beg families.'
Daily Mail, 6 October 2000
© Atlantic Syndication

Chapter 10 'The Dunblane Tragedy: why?' *Scotland on Sunday,*
17 March 1996
© Scotsman Publications Limited

Index